Preserved Military Vehicles

Keith Jenkinson

Rochester Press Transport Books

ISBN 0 946379 08 4

Printed and bound in England by Staples Printers Rochester
Limited at The Stanhope Press.

Published by Rochester Press Ltd., 38 High Street,
Chatham, Kent.

INTRODUCTION

Although in general terms the preservation of commercial and military vehicles has only just reached its twenty-fifth birthday, some areas of transport conservation have been apparent for more than twice that length of time. As far as the collecting together of military vehicles is concerned this began more than fifty years ago and is largely due to the foresight shown by what was then the Royal Tank Corps. In 1924 they began to preserve some of the early tanks built for use in world war I and during the following year they started what has now become the famous Tank Museum at Bovington. Although in the years that followed, numerous tanks and experimental vehicles were added to this growing collection, it was not until 1947 that the museum was opened to the public. By this time the museum was under the control of the Royal Armoured Corps which had been formed in 1939, swallowing up the Royal Tank Corps in the process. The Imperial War Museum had by this time started a much smaller but equally interesting collection and thus the preservation of military vehicles was underway. The vast majority of the vehicles saved for posterity were of the armoured type and it was not until much later that soft-skinned vehicles began to attract interest.

With large numbers of military vehicles being released after the end of world war II for civilian use, there was still a good representative selection available in the late 'fifties and early 'sixties and it was these that the private sector of the preservation movement began to collect. Each one acquired was de-civilianised and returned to its former military condition and by the end of the 'sixties a wide variety of makes and models were safely being cared for in various parts of Britain. To these were added numerous vehicles bought direct out of military service and indeed, this is continuing today. Whilst most of those preserved originated from British or American military forces, interesting examples from Germany, Russia and many other countries have also been added to the growing numbers in preservation, thus portraying a wide ranging history.

Unlike preserved civilian vehicles, many of the military ones being restored have not yet been given civilian registration numbers and therefore this book differs in some ways from those relating to lorries and buses, previously published. Some vehicles are shown in the pages which follow listed by their civilian registration numbers, others are identified by their military numbers and some are listed without any identification marks. It is appreciated that this may in some cases cause difficulty to readers, but spaces have been left to allow these numbers to be inserted when the restorations are completed and a civilian number is issued.

Although the Historic Commercial Vehicle Society caters for all types of preserved commercial and military vehicles, there are numerous clubs throughout Britain which cater solely for those concerned with the conservation of military vehicles and equipment, and it is to the latter that most military enthusiasts belong.

Compiling this book has been no easy task and I am deeply indebted to numerous people who have given me help, and in particular to David Game, Barry Webb and John Edwards whose advice and assistance has been invaluable. I would also extend my sincere thanks to all those who have supplied me with and permitted me to use their photographs in this work and finally to my wife who has allowed me to bury the lounge and furniture beneath mountains of papers for many, many months without complaint.

1

Whilst I have endeavoured to make this book as complete as possible, there are no doubt some military vehicles which have escaped all my efforts to include and I would therefore welcome details of these so that they may be included in any future revised edition of this title.

Keith A. Jenkinson
Queensbury, Bradford.
January 1983.

A1 E1

The A1 E1 was an experimental heavy tank designed by Vickers Armstrongs. The pilot model was delivered in 1926 and was 25 ft. 5 in. long and armed with 1 × 3 pdr. QF gun with Vickers MGs in its subsidiary turrets. It was powered by an Armstrong Siddeley V12 air-cooled petrol engine of 398 bhp. Of advanced design, the A1 E1 carried a crew of 8. No further tanks of this model were built however owing to the cost of production.

Example Preserved.

	1926	Tank	Brit. Army	RAC Museum, Bovington.

AEC MATADOR

Introduced in 1939, the AEC 0853 model, named Matador, was a 4 × 4 vehicle with a wheelbase of 12 ft. 7½ in. of forward control layout. Powered by an AEC 7.58 litre 6-cylinder oil engine, it had a 4-speed gearbox, single dry plate clutch and a rear axle which could be of the double reduction spiral bevel or worm type. The original artillery tractors had air pressure assisted Lockheed hydraulic brakes but later, the Matador was built with full air brakes. A batch destined for shipment to Norway were fitted with AEC 6-cylinder petrol engines and were thus designated 853. Numerous different types of bodywork was used including artillery tractor, signals van, tanker and flat platform. Production of the Matador ended in October 1945 by which time 9,620 had been built.

Examples Preserved.

	1939	Recovery	Brit. Army	Kilby, Wimborne
SGF911V	1939	Recovery	Brit. Army	Nicholson, Chippenham
	1939	Artillery Tractor	Brit. Army	Davies, London
	1939	Artillery Tractor	Brit. Army	Cleaver, Charlbury
TAN494F	1942	Artillery Tractor	Brit. Army	Franklin, Ware
TFP858R	1942	Artillery Tractor	Brit. Army	Hughes
	1942	Artillery Tractor	Brit. Army	Springhall, Burton on Trent
		Artillery Tractor	Brit. Army	Strathallan Museum, Perthshire
12RD24		Artillery Tractor	Brit. Army	Imperial War Museum, Duxford
LDM784	1943	Artillery Tractor	Brit. Army	Rivett, Leatherhead
GNR720D	1943		Royal Navy	Mankin, Heddon on the Wall

AEC Mk.II ARMOURED CAR

Preserved at Bovington is this AEC Mk.II Armoured Car of 1943 vintage.

Replacing the AEC Mk.I Armoured Car early in 1943, the Mk.II was a 4 × 4 vehicle which used many of the components used in the AEC Matador artillery tractor. Powered by an AEC 158 bhp. 6-cylinder diesel engine mounted at the rear, it had a weight of 12.7 tons. Designed to carry a crew of 4, it was armed with 1 × 6 pdr. gun and 1 × 7.92 mm. co-axial Besa MG. Having electrical power and hand traverse for the turret, the 6 pdr. (57 mm.) gun was not considered adequate and the Mk.II was discountinued in favour of the Mk.III early in 1944.

Example Preserved.

1943	Armoured Car	Brit. Army	RAC Museum, Bovington

AEC 850

Of somewhat antique appearance is the AEC R6T/850 of which AMP80 is the only example with personnel carrier bodywork known to be preserved.

(C. Pearce)

The AEC 850 was a 6 × 6 artillery tractor first built by AEC in 1929 after their takeover of FWD, the manufacturer who first introduced the R6T/850. Of forward control layout, the AEC 850 was powered by an AEC 6-cylinder petrol engine of 6126 cc. with a bore and stroke of 100 mm. × 130 mm. Transmission was via a 4-speed gearbox with 2-speed transfer box whilst the brakes were hydraulically operated. The 850, which was built with a 10 ft. 0 in. wheelbase, could be fitted with either artillery tractor or recovery tractor bodywork and was used almost exclusively by the RAOC. It remained in production until 1936.

Examples Preserved.

AMP80	1930	Personnel Carrier	Brit. Army	Miles, Shaftesbury
		Gun Tractor	Brit. Army	Lambe, Fenstanton.

ALBION AM463

Introduced originally for use as an ambulance, the Albion AM463 first appeared in 1934. Of normal control layout with a wheelbase of 12 ft. 0 in., this 4 × 2 2-ton model was powered by an Albion 4-cylinder 65.5 bhp. petrol engine and used a 4-speed gearbox. Of the 1,900 AM463 chassis supplied, a number were fitted with GS, crane, van, tractor or tanker bodies for use by the RAF, production ending in 1941.

Example Preserved.

JMV149	1937	Ambulance	Robinson, North Mimms

5

ALBION CX22S

UTP68K, a preserved Albion CX22 gun tractor now restored to its former glory at Duxford.

(D. Game)

The Albion CX22S was introduced in February 1944, being a normal control 6 × 4 model with a wheelbase of 14 ft. 8 in. Classified as a heavy artillery tractor it was powered by an Albion 6-cylinder diesel engine of 100 bhp. and was fitted with a 4-speed gearbox and 2-speed transfer box. The CX22S was given a well-floor body with crew compartment at the front. It remained in production until 1946.

Examples Preserved.

UTP68K	1944	Artillery Tractor	Brit. Army	T.Corbin, Rush Green
	1944	Artillery Tractor	Brit. Army	McIntyre, Sorn Castle

ALBION FT11N

Entering production in February 1940, the Albion FT11N was a 4 × 4 3-ton truck of forward control layout. Having a wheelbase of 12 ft. 0 in. it was powered by an Albion 6-cylinder, 4.57 litre engine of the EN280A type whilst transmission was via a 4-speed gearbox with 2-speed transfer box. The brakes were mechanically operated with servo assistance. Whilst the majority of FT11's were fitted with GS bodywork, some equipped as Kitchens, Machinery and Offices etc. The FT11 remained in production until August 1944.

Example Preserved.

G/S Cargo	Swainson, Romford

ALBION FT15N

Introduced in 1945, the Albion FT15N was a 6×6 Field Artillery tractor of semi-forward control layout. Having a wheelbase of 12 ft. 6 in. it was powered by an Albion 6-cylinder 95 bhp. engine and was fitted with a 4-speed gearbox with 2-speed transfer box. Of the low-silhouette type, it had a Turner 8-ton worm drive winch. A variant produced was the FT15NW which was fully water-proofed.
Production of the FT15N and FT15NW ended later in 1945 after only 150 had been built.

Example Preserved.

	1945	Artillery Tractor	Brit. Army	Haylock, Maldon

ALBION FT103N

The 3-ton Albion FT103N was basically the civilian 'Clansman' adapted for military use. Of forward control layout it was of 6×4 configuration and had a wheelbase of 11 ft. 9½ in. It used an Albion 4-cylinder diesel engine of 75 bhp. and had a 5-speed gearbox and vacuum assisted hydraulic brakes. Introduced for military use in 1949 it remained in production until 1952 and was fitted with various specialist bodies for use by the Army.

Examples Preserved.

	1950	Mobile Workshop	Brit. Army	Jackson, Wormingford
XEL416S	1952	Mobile Workshop	Brit. Army	Britton, Kingsway

ALVIS FV610

On display to passers-by outside Bassingbourne Barracks is this Alvis built FV610.

(K. A. Jenkinson)

Built as an armoured command carrier, the Alvis FV610 was based on the Saracen introduced in 1952 but had a higher, wider hull. A 6×6 vehicle with equally spaced axles it had a 10 ft. 0 in. wheelbase and was powered by a Rolls Royce B80 Mk.6A 8-cylinder petrol engine of 170 bhp. this being front mounted. Semi-automatic transmission was fitted with 5-forward and 5-reverse gears. The FV610 remained in production until the early 'seventies.

Example Preserved.

01DA48   1957   Armoured carrier   Brit. Army   Bassingbourne Barracks

AMX-13

Originating from the French Army, this AMX-13 tank dates from 1954.

(K. A. Jenkinson)

The French built AMK-13 light airportable tank entered production in 1952 after various prototypes had been built in 1948/9. Its SOFAM 8-cylinder petrol engine is mounted in the front of the hull to the right, and the AMX-13 carries a crew of 3. It is 15 ft. 0 in. long, 8 ft. 2 in. wide and 7 ft. 7 in. high and is armed with 1×75 mm. gun and 1×7.5 mm. or 7.62 mm. co-axial MG whilst 2 smoke dischargers are incorporated to each side of the turret. Although at first the AMX-13 was not equipped with infra-red night driving lights, later production models were given this valuable equipment. The AMX-13 still remains in production today with over 4,500 having been built to date.

Example Preserved.

2480316   1954   Airportable Tank. French Army RAC Museum, Bovington

ARCHER

The Archer was a self-propelled gun, being basically a Valentine chassis with an open topped superstructure over the fighting compartment. The pilot model was completed in April 1943 and the first production model delivered in March 1944. Vickers built 665 Archers, some of which remained in service until the mid 'sixties. Its rear pointing gun was a 17 pdr. OQF whilst secondary armament was provided by a .303 cal. Besa MG (AA). Powered by a GMC 165 hp. diesel engine, the Archer was 21 ft. 11¼ in. long, 8 ft. 7½ in. wide and 7 ft. 4½ in. high.

Example Preserved.

1944 S.P. Gun   Brit. Army   RAC Museum, Bovington

AUSTIN CHAMP

One of many Austin Champs now preserved, 824GUL was built in 1953.

(K. A. Jenkinson)

The Austin Champ entered production in the autumn of 1952. It was a 4×4 normal control vehicle used by the armed forces as a ¼ ton utility. Having a wheelbase of 7 ft. 0 in. it was powered by a Rolls Royce 4-cylinder 2.66 litre petrol engine and had a 5-speed gearbox and hypoid final drive. Its brakes were hydraulically operated and acted on all 4 wheels. The Champ remained in production until 1958.

Examples Preserved.

NNR359G	1950	Utility	Brit. Army	Lewis, Hinckley
	1952	Utility	Brit. Army	Strand, Christchurch
824GUL	1953	Utility	Brit. Army	Jones, Bradford on Avon
	1954	Utility	Brit. Army	Buckley & Jackson, Croydon
	1954	Utility	Brit. Army	Elvis, Water Orton
	1955	Utility	Brit. Army	Miller, Gosport
YUT187H	1955	Utility	Brit. Army	Wardle, Cheadle
		Utility	Brit. Army	Stephenson, Gateshead
		Utility	Brit. Army	Hardy, Newcastle on Tyne
		Utility	Brit. Army	Wilson, Hexham
		Utility	Brit. Army	Haydon, St. Ives
		Utility	Brit. Army	Dodds, Hexham
		Utility	Brit. Army	White, Sacriston
		Utility	Brit. Army	Sieyeking, West Buckland
		Utility	Brit. Army	Sneddon, Sunderland
		Utility	Brit. Army	Fothergill, Newcastle on Tyne
		Utility	Brit. Army	Moulson, Bradford
		Utility	Brit. Army	West, Biggleswade
		Utility	Brit. Army	Plews, Middlesbrough
		Utility	Brit. Army	Norrie, Newcastle on Tyne
RVO949F	1955	Utility	Brit. Army	Whitehead, Sacriston
CWF763K	1955	Utility	Brit. Army	Private Owner

AUSTIN G/YG

Pictured at a rally in Scotland, Austin utility CSH512 wears its Army markings in true military style.
(K. A. Jenkinson)

Introduced in 1939, the Austin G/YG 4 × 2 light utility was based on the pre-war Austin 10 car chassis. Being of normal control layout with a wheelbase of 7 ft. 10¾ in., it is powered by an Austin 4-cylinder petrol engine of 9.99 hp. with a bore and stroke of 2.4995 in. × 3.5 in. Transmission is via a 4-speed synchromesh gearbox and single dry plate clutch to a spiral bevel rear axle whilst the brakes are mechanically operated, acting on all wheels. A pick-up type body with canvas tilt is fitted, the spare wheel being carried in a recess on the cab roof. The G/YG was produced until the end of 1944.

Examples Preserved.

		Utility	Brit. Army	Bowman, Blaydon
PER766	1939	Utility	Brit. Army	Groombridge, Heathfield
277HPU	1940	Utility	Brit. Army	Harris
FDD436	1941	Utility		Jarman, Stroud
CSH512	1942	Utility	Brit. Army	Cremer, Edinburgh
XTA899	1942	Utility	Brit. Army	Theobald, Warnham
KJU393	1943	Utility	Royal Navy	Willis, New Haw
NRP658	1943	Utility		Marshall, Northants
UCG71	1943	Utility		Clutterbuck, Bookham
	1943	Utility		Marray, Belfast
	1943	Utility		J. Marchant, Milton Keynes
	1943	Utility		Colvin, London
	1943	Utility		Gates, London
	1943	Utility		Worthing
DUN660	1943	Utility	Brit. Army	Brown, Preston

AUSTIN K2/Y

Restored as an Army ambulance, HMO105K was built in 1942.

(K. A. Jenkinson)

The Austin K2/Y ambulance was introduced in 1939. A 2-ton 4×2 model, it has a wheelbase of 11 ft. 2 in. Powered by an Austin 6-cylinder petrol engine of 3.46 litres capacity with a bore and stroke of 3.35 in.×4 in., it has a 4-speed gearbox, single dry plate clutch and fully floating rear axle with spiral bevel final drive. Lockheed hydraulic brakes act on all wheels and its ambulance bodywork was of the four stretcher type. 13,102 were built before production ended in 1945, and canteen bodywork could also be fitted.

Examples Preserved.

JMW106	1939	Ambulance	Brit. Army	Passey, Newbury
SED948	1940	Ambulance	Brit. Army	Mollo & Brownlow, London
FUF48	1941	Ambulance	Brit. Army	Warnham War Museum
SGS947	1941	Ambulance	Brit. Army	Harper, Attleborough
992EPW	1941	Ambulance	Brit. Army	Smith, Ipswich
	1941	Ambulance		Maddocks, Shrewsbury
	1941	Ambulance	Brit. Army	Bloomfield, Somerset
	1941	Ambulance		Jones, Ludlow
GLT339	1941	Ambulance	Brit. Army	Bowman, Blaydon
A1736688	1942	Ambulance	Brit. Army	Webb, Bishops Stortford
RDP807	1942	Ambulance	Brit. Army	Venners, Reading
	1942	Ambulance	Brit. Army	Holmes, Falmouth
GXW714	1942	Ambulance	Brit. Army	Hayters, Macclesfield
	1942	Ambulance	Brit. Army	Robinson, Burton Latimer
	1942	Canteen		Beal, Surrey
HMO105K	1943	Ambulance	Brit. Army	Oxford Military Vehicle Assoc.
KYN896	1943	Ambulance	Brit. Army	Gates, Dorset
TEP846	1943	Ambulance	Brit. Army	Parish, Oswestry
	1943	Ambulance		Twycross, Northants
JXW780	1943	Ambulance	Brit. Army	Mutch, Aberlady
JUU497	1943	Ambulance	Brit. Army	Cook, Lockerbie
JXN780	1944	Ambulance		Private Owner
109OCX	1944	Ambulance	Brit. Army	Mann, Lamanva
	1944	Canteen	Brit. Army	Offord, Christchurch

AUSTIN K3

GUU114 is an Austin K3 with Civil Defence bodywork.

(D. Game)

Introduced in 1939, the Austin K3 was a 3-ton 4×2 truck of normal control layout. Given a wheelbase of 13 ft. 1 in. it was fitted with an Austin 6-cylinder 26.88 hp. petrol engine, 4-speed gearbox and Lockheed hydraulic type brakes. Although the most common type of body fitted was the GS, the Austin K3 also received other types of bodywork including tipper and workshop. 17,097 were built before production ended in the summer of 1945.

Examples Preserved.

	1941	Canteen Van		Warnham War Museum
SVE156	1942	G/S Cargo	Brit. Army	Webb & Seabrook, Duxford
GUU114	1942	Van	Civil Defence	Imperial War Museum, Duxford.
	1943	G/S Cargo	Brit. Army	Townend, Haverhill
	1943	G/S Cargo	Brit. Army	Franklin, Ashwell
	1943	G/S Cargo	Brit. Army	Robinson, Burton Latimer

AUSTIN K5

Awaiting restoration is this World War II Austin K5 cargo truck.

(P. Isaac)

The Austin K5, introduced in 1941 was a 4 × 4, 3-ton model built as a general services load carrier. Fitted with an Austin 3.99 litre 6-cylinder engine, it was of forward control layout and had a wheelbase of 12 ft. 0 in. Its transmission was via a single dry plate clutch and 4-speed gearbox with 2-speed transfer box whilst its brakes were of the servo assisted hydraulic type. A total of 12,280 K5's were built before production ended in 1945.

Examples Preserved.

NGF621P	1941	Breakdown Tender		MT Pres. Group, Croydon
	1942	G/S Cargo	Brit. Army	Bloomfield, Taunton
	1942	G/S Cargo	Brit. Army	Maddocks, Shrewsbury
86732	1943	G/S Cargo	Brit. Army	Lovegrove & Walmsley, Duxford
	1943	G/S Cargo	Brit. Army	Issac, Devon
LS7725	1944	G/S Cargo	Brit. Army	Bowman, Blaydon

AUSTIN K6

Carrying the remains of a generator body, Austin K6 ZD4998 awaits restoration by its new owners.
(M. Corcoran)

Introduced at the beginning of 1944, the Austin K6 was a 3-ton 6 × 4 model which replaced the K4. Of normal control layout, it was given a wheelbase of 12 ft. 9 in. Its engine was an Austin 3.99 litre 6-cylinder petrol unit whilst transmission was via a 4-speed gearbox with 2-speed transfer box. Hydraulic servo assisted brakes were fitted. Built chiefly for the RAF, the K6 could be fitted with various types of special purpose bodywork including a breakdown gantry (K6/A), signals van (K6/ZB) or general services. It remained in production until 1945.

Examples Preserved.

K6/A	FUF49	1944	Breakdown Gantry	Brit. Army	Warnham War Museum
K6/ZB	ZD4998	1944	Generator	Irish Army	TMS, Castleruddery
K6/ZB		1944	Balloon Winch	RAF	Imperial War Museum, Duxford
K6/XB		1944	Radar Repair Van	RAF	Brand & Haydon, Duxford

AUSTIN K9

The Austin K9 was a 4×4 vehicle which could be fitted with a variety of bodywork for military use. The vehicle depicted here carries a wireless house body.

(K. A. Jenkinson)

Introduced in 1953 the Austin K9 was a 1-ton 4×4 vehicle of normal control layout. Having a wheelbase of 11 ft. 5¼ in., the K9 was powered by an Austin 6-cylinder petrol engine of 90 bhp. and had a 4-speed gear box and hydraulic brakes. A number of versions were built for military use including the FV16001 with cargo bodywork, FV16002 fitted for wireless, FV16003 wireless, FV16004 radio repair, FV16005 Ambulance and FV16009 water tanker. A civilian version was also built, this being a 4×2 variant known as the Loadstar and both this and the military K9 were discontinued in 1956 when they were replaced by updated models.

Examples Preserved.

	1952	Wireless	Brit. Army	Lane, Ripley, Derby
TAA299T	1952		Brit. Army	Hanson, Stalbridge
	1953	Wireless	Brit. Army	Alexander, Bournemouth
	1956	Wireless	Brit. Army	Foster, Chester le Street

AUSTIN SEVEN

The Austin Seven was used as a scout car. HX6792 illustrated here typifies this diminutive type of vehicle.

(R. F. Mack)

First introduced in 1924, the Austin Seven was a normal control type 4×2 vehicle with a 2½ cwt. payload capacity. With a wheelbase of 6 ft. 3 in., it used an Austin 7.8 hp. 4-cylinder petrol engine, and had a 3-speed gearbox and bevel rear axle. Its brakes were mechanically operated and acted on all 4 wheels. During 1931 its wheelbase was extended to 6 ft. 9 in. and in 1932 it was given a 4-speed gearbox. The brakes underwent change in 1936 becoming hydraulically operated and the Austin Seven, used by the armed forces as a light utility, was discontinued in 1937.

Example Preserved.

HX6792   1931   Scout Car   Brit. Army   Hodge, Windsor

BANTAM 40BRC

The Bantam 40BRC jeep was a 5 cwt. 4×4 command reconnaissance vehicle of normal control layout. First built in 1941 it had a 6 ft. 7½ in. wheelbase and was powered by a Continental 4-cylinder petrol engine of 45 bhp. Transmission was via a 3-speed gearbox with 2-speed transfer box and the brakes were mechanically operated. The Bantam was the first 'jeep' to appear in Britain and before production ended later in 1941, a total of 2,675 were built, most of which went to the UK or USSR.

Example Preserved.

1941   Jeep   Brit. Army   Hart, Sussex

AUTO UNION MUNGA

Now preserved at Duxford is this Auto Union 4×4 of the post Second World War period.

(D. Game)

The Auto Union 'Munga' made its debut in 1955 as a 4×4, 4-seater field car. Given a wheelbase of 2.0 m. it used an Auto Union AU1000 3-cylinder petrol engine of 980 cc. and was fitted with a 4-speed gearbox with 2-speed transfer box (permanent all-wheel drive was fitted to all except those built during 1955-56). Hydraulic brakes were fitted and the 'Munga' remained in production until 1968 by which time around 55,000 had been built. A civilian version was also available.

Examples Preserved.

		Field Car	Ger. Army	Imperial War Museum, Duxford
PWY462M	1959	Field Car	Ger. Army	Rowlands, Wetherby

BEDFORD K

Introduced as a civilian vehicle in the autumn of 1939, the Bedford K range was of normal control layout and had a wheelbase of 10 ft. 0 in. Powered by a Bedford 6-cylinder petrol engine of 27.34 hp. it had a 4-speed gearbox and Lockheed hydraulic brakes. Production was suspended from 1940 to 1945 and it was not until 1946 that the K was introduced into military service as a 4×2 30 cwt. model. The KC was a chassis cab that could be fitted with an assortment of bodywork whilst the KD was a dropside GS truck. The K range remained in production until 1953.

Examples Preserved.

KC		1944		Brit. Army	Mapperson, Coventry
KC	WXE168		Wireless	MOD	Gray, Hanworth
KD		1939	Crew Tender	RAF	Owen, Stroud
KD	AOG163B	1951	G/S Cargo	Brit. Army	Smith, Newbury

BEDFORD MW

Seen here without number plates, Bedford MWD VBW98 has been authentically restored to its original Army condition.

(K. A. Jenkinson)

The Bedford MW was a 15 cwt. 4×2 vehicle of normal control layout. Having a wheelbase of 8 ft. 3 in., it was powered by a Bedford 3.5 litre 6-cylinder petrol engine with a bore and stroke of 85.72 mm. $\times$ 101.6 mm. Transmission was via a 4-speed gearbox, single dry plate clutch and fully floating spiral bevel rear axle whilst the brakes which act on all four wheels were of the Lockheed hydraulic type. First introduced in 1939, six variants were built, these being:

MWC Water Tanker   MWR Fitted for Wireless
MWD General Service   MWT Anti-Tank Gun Tractor
MWG Gun Mounting   MWV General Service Van

Early models of the MW had open cabs, small folding windscreens and canvas side panels, later models being equipped with full windscreens, metal doors and detachable side screens. The MW remained in production until 1945.

Examples Preserved.

MWC		Water Tanker	Blyth, Holt
MWC	1939	Water Tanker	Brit. Army	Oldreive, Shanklin
MWC 85YS56	1942	Water Tanker	Brit. Army	Sneller, Dover
MWC JNH426N		Water Tanker	Robinson, Burton Latimer
MWD EMR246	1939	G/S Truck	Bowman, Blayton
MWD OLC951P	1939	G/S Truck	Mayer, Cheshunt
MWD TVS874R	1939	G/S Truck	Bygraves, Bedford
MWD HDD170	1940	G/S Truck	Buckland, Pagenhill
MWD YNJ8	1940	G/S Truck	Groombridge, Heathfield
MWD HCC104	1941	G/S Truck	Whitehouse, Bishops Cleeve

MWD	1941	G/S Truck		Grange Cavern Museum, Holywell
MWD MBW267	1942	G/S Truck	Brit. Army	Moulson, Bradford
MWD	1942	G/S Truck		Brett, Wisbech
MWD	1942	G/S Truck		Pretty, Partridge Green
MWD VBW98	1942	G/S Truck	Brit. Army	Mann, Lamanva
MWD 9609VT	1942	G/S Truck		Private Owner
MWD MJK370	1943	G/S Truck	RAF	Bone, Newhaven
MWD PJU771R	1943	G/S Truck		Beddall, Iver
MWD TEP843	1943	G/S Truck	Brit. Army	Levee, Stocksfield
MWD 9103WF	1943	G/S Truck		Hall, Durham
MWD	1944	G/S Truck		Fortnum, Rugby
MWD 2592554	1944	G/S Truck		Warnham War Museum
MWD UHH600		G/S Truck		Mankin, Heddon on the Wall
MWD	1943	G/S Truck	RAF	RAF Museum, Henlow
MWR YMR58	1940	Wireless	RAF	Jarman, Stroud
MWR GDF19	1941	Wireless	RAF	Owen, Stroud
MWR 34RD44	1943	Wireless		Brook, Houghton
MWR TJB101G	1943	Wireless	Brit. Army	Passey, Newbury
MWR 3279PG	1943	Wireless		Mitchell
MWR	1943	Wireless		Pring, Hants
MWR 25252409		Wireless		Webb, Duxford
MW VVF657S	1942			Reynolds
MW JPL754N	1943			Poole, Aldershot
MW 392RAE	1943			Mansell, Pershore
MW DDP727	1943			Private Owner
MW KHP69N	1943			Private Owner
MW OSO93R	1942			Private Owner
MW RAY431M	1943			39/40 Group
MW GYY941	1942			Private Owner
MW 805FUF	1942			Private Owner
MW 990EPW	1943			Harper, Attleborough
MW	1943			Rowland, London
MW	1943			Finlay, Aberdeen
MW	1943			Houldershaw, Boston

BEDFORD OL

MDF475F, a post-war Bedford OLBC authentically restored to its British Army condition.
(K. A. Jenkinson)

Launched in 1939 as a civilian model the Bedford OL was a 3-5 ton 4×2 vehicle of normal control layout with a wheelbase of 13 ft. 1 in. It was given a Bedford 27.34 hp. 6-cylinder petrol engine and 4-speed gearbox and had Lockheed hydraulic brakes. During the period 1940-45, production of the OL was suspended and in 1946 the OL was built for military service as well as for civilian use. The OLAC was a 3-4 ton chassis/cab built for fitting with various types of bodywork, the OLAD being the dropside GS version. The OL continued to be built until 1953.

Examples Preserved.

OLBC	MDF475F	1952	G/S Cargo	Brit. Army	Bradshaw, Ashbourne
OLBC	JAT358D		G/S Cargo	Brit. Army	Private Owner
OLBC	JKH549D		G/S Cargo	Brit. Army	Private Owner
OLBD			Tipper		Stewart, Sheffield

BEDFORD OW

First introduced in 1941, the OW series was offered with a choice of wheelbase, the OWS having a measurement of 9 ft. 3 in., the OWL being 13 ft. 1 in. The Bedford OW was a 5-ton 4×2 type with normal control layout and used a Bedford 27.3 hp. 6-cylinder petrol engine, 4-speed gearbox and Lockeed hydraulic brakes. The OWS was most common in military use fitted with tipper bodywork (designed OWST), the OWL being used in less numbers and fitted with GS bodywork. The OW series continued in production until 1945.

Examples Preserved.

OWST		1941	Tipper	Royal Navy	Haylock, Malden
OWST	898JTE	1942	Tipper	Royal Navy	Groarke, Stockton Heath
OWST		1942	Chassis/cab	RAF	Pretty, Partridge Green
OWST	EVE848		Tipper	Brit. Army	Wallman, Cambridge
OWL	JDF428	1942	F/P Lorry	Brit. Army	Private Owner

21

BEDFORD OX

Bedford produced several models during World War II, differing only in their carrying capacity and overall dimensions. This OXD 30-cwt variant is fitted with general service bodywork as supplied to the British Army. Alongside it is a contemporary Hillman staff car.

(K. A. Jenkinson)

The Bedford OX was a normal control 4×2 model in the 30 cwt. range. Introduced in 1939 it had a wheelbase of 9 ft. 3 in. and was fitted with a Bedford 6-cylinder 27.34 hp. petrol engine, 4-speed gearbox and hydraulic brakes. A number of variants were built, the OXC being available as a mobile canteen or as a tractor unit used to draw a Scammell or Tasker semi-trailer of the dropside lorry, flat platform lorry, petrol tanker or bus type, the OXD being a general service truck. The OX series remained in production until 1945.

Examples Preserved.

OXC	1942	Tractor		Mann, Lamanva
OXC GXE890	1943	Tractor	Atomic Com-	
			mission	Carnall, Barkby
OXC GNV824D	1943	Tractor	RAF	Webb, Duxford
OXC		Tractor		Baddows, Hants
OXC		Tractor		Mankin, Heddon on the Wall
OXC		Tractor		Tarrant, Waltham
OXD	1939	G/S Truck		Mankin, Heddon on the Wall
OXD XPC75N	1939	G/S Truck		Taylor, Croydon

BEDFORD OY

First appearing in 1939 the Bedford OY was a normal control 3-ton model of
4×2 configuration. Powered by a 3.5 litre 6-cylinder Bedford petrol engine, it
had a 4-speed gearbox and hydraulic brakes. The OY had a wheelbase of
13 ft. 1 in. and was built in two forms, the OYC having tanker bodywork with a
carrying capacity of 350 gallons (this was increased to 500 gallons in 1943)
camouflaged with a canvas tilt on a detachable superstructure whilst the OYD
had GS body work. Production of the OY continued until 1945.

Examples Preserved.

OYC	424NPT	1942	Tanker	Brit. Army	Levee, Stocksfield
OYC	AY785	1942	Tanker	RAF	Priddle, Cross & Shepherd, Farnham
OYC			Tanker		Mann, Lamanva
OYC			Tanker		Webb & Seabrook, Bishops Stortford
OYC			Tanker	RAF	RAF Museum, Henlow
OYC	VGV648		Tanker		Flack, Coleford
OYD	9143BP	1940	G/S Truck	Brit. Army	Bedford Pres. Club, Bedfont
OYD	JUV543	1940	G/S Truck	Brit. Army	Owen, Stroud
OYD	986DWD	1941	G/S Truck	Brit. Army	Bradshaw, Ashbourne
OYD	FHC533	1942	G/S Truck	Brit. Army	Oxford Military Vehicle Assoc.
OYD		1942	G/S Truck	Brit. Army	Hounsell, Dorchester
OYD	FJK191	1942	G/S Truck	Brit. Army	Brooks, Old Heathfield
OYD	SWH559S	1943	G/S Truck	Brit. Army	Slater, Oldham
OYD			G/S Truck	Brit. Army	West, Southampton
OYD			G/S Truck	Brit. Army	Pearce, Holywell
OYD			G/S Truck	Brit. Army	Walker, Boston
OYD			G/S Truck	Brit. Army	RCT, Plymouth
OYD	SJR581		G/S Truck	Brit. Army	Mankin, Heddon on the Wall
OYD			G/S Truck	Brit. Army	Cordiner, Loughborough
OYD	868DER		G/S Truck	Brit. Army	Webb & Seabrook, Bishops Stortford
OYD			G/S Truck	Brit. Army	McIntyre, Sorn Castle
OYD	SCE119	1944	G/S Truck	Brit. Army	Walman, Cambridge
OYD	487LUY	1944	G/S Truck	Brit. Army	Groombridge, Heathfield
OYD	KCE440P		Tipper	Brit. Army	Denyer, Littlebury
OYD	L2124591		G/S Truck	Brit. Army	Houldershaw, Boston
OYD	HGV569E	1945	G/S Truck	Brit. Army	Little, Mansfield
OYD			Airfield Sweeper	RAF	Marchant, Milton Keynes

BEDFORD QL

This 1942 Bedford QLR fitted with wireless house bodywork has been beautifully restored to authentic condition.

(K. A. Jenkinson collection)

Introduced in 1941, the Bedford QL was a 4×4 forward control 3-ton vehicle. Powered by a Bedford 6-cylinder petrol engine of 3519 cc. with a bore and stroke of 85.72 mm. × 101.6 mm., it had a 4-speed gearbox with 2-speed transfer box and was given a wheelbase of 11 ft. 11 in. Vacuum servo assisted Lockheed hydraulic brakes were fitted acting on all 4 wheels. Various types of bodywork were fitted, each type having its own designation as follows:

QLB AA Tractor (Bofors)	QLT Troop Carrier
QLC Petrol Tanker	QLR Wireless
QLC Truck-Tractor with	QL miscellaneous (Fire Tender,
semi-trailer	Workshop, Office etc.
QLD Cargo GS	

The QL remained in production until 1945 by which time 52,245 had been built.

Examples Preserved.

QLB	288480		Bofors	RAF	Smith, Duxford
QLB			Bofors		Shuker, Salop
QLC	THX668F	1941	Petrol Tanker	Brit. Army	Beddall, Iver
QLC	THX775F	1941	Petrol Tanker		Beddall, Iver
QLC	RAF2581		Petrol Tanker	RAF	Corbin, Duxford
QLC			Portee		Mayer, Cheshunt
QLC			Petrol Tanker		Mosquito Museum, London Colney
QLC	TMT653F	1942	Petrol Tanker		Beddall, Iver
QLC	TOO234N	1943	Petrol Tanker	RAF	Corbin, Romford
QLC			Petrol Tanker		Smith, Andrews Field
QLC			Petrol Tanker		Reynolds, Norfolk
QLD	L5241923		G/S Truck		Webb, Duxford

QLD			G/S Truck		Tarrant, Gt. Waltham
QLD	YNJ968P	1942	G/S Truck	Brit. Army	James, Iver
QLD			G/S Truck		Purser, New Wimpole
QLD	YNP956R		G/S Truck	Brit. Army	Beddall, Iver
QLD			G/S Truck		Blyth, Holt
QLD	XWT257G	1943	G/S Truck		Williams, Fordwells
QLR		1941	Signals	Brit. Army	Grange Cavern Museum, Holywell
QLR			Wireless	Brit. Army	Parish, Salop
QLR			Wireless		Paris, Bishops Stortford
QLR	OYG203F	1942	Wireless	Brit. Army	Wardale, Ripon
QLR	04YX83	1942	Wireless		Binnie, Iver Heath
QLR	ULM6F	1942	Wireless	Brit. Army	Oxhey Venture Group, Pinner
QLR	VBH501N	1942	Office	Brit. Army	Beddall, Iver
QLR			Wireless		Parker, Sussex
QLR	LPU30K	1943	Command Post	Brit. Army	Denton, Hants
QLR	TMT756F	1943	Wireless	Brit. Army	Webb & Seabrook, Duxford
QLR	TLE135R	1943	Office	Brit. Army	Beddall, Iver
QLR		1943	Wireless	Brit. Army	Rushton, Devon
QLR	23YX78	1944	Machine Shop	Brit. Army	SEME, Bordon
QLR	JPE12K	1944	Wireless		Private Owner
QLR	OPP41M	1944	Wireless	Brit. Army	Beddall, Iver
QLR			Wireless	Brit. Army	Sayer, Suffolk
QLR			Wireless	Brit. Army	Pearce, Clwyd
QLR		1944	Wireless	Brit. Army	Springall, Burton on Trent
QLR	SJT583M	1944	Wireless	Brit. Army	Private Owner
QLR	RW2121		Command Post	Brit. Army	Gray, Worthing
QLT	URB772	1940	Troop Carrier	Royal Navy	Mankin, Heddon on the Wall
QLT	RPE500E	1942	Troop Carrier	Brit. Army	Beddall, Iver
QLT	767FGF	1944	Troop Carrier	Brit. Army	Levee, Stocksfield
QLT			Troop Carrier	Brit. Army	Reynolds, Norfolk
QLT		1944	Troop Carrier	Brit. Army	Mann, Lamanva
QL	FPG151B			Brit. Army	Private Owner
QL	J1321			Brit. Army	Private Owner, Jersey
QL				Brit. Army	Foley, London
QL	HBH102C	1943	Breakdown Truck		WETC, Winkleigh
QL				Brit. Army	Johnson, Hants
QL		1943		Brit. Army	Moulson, Bradford

BEDFORD SAG

Based on the Bedford S-series, the SAG was introduced in 1951. The SAG was a tractor unit of 4×2 configuration with forward control layout designed for use with a 'Queen Mary' 5-ton semi-trailer. Powered by a Bedford 6-cylinder petrol engine of 113 bhp. it has a wheelbase of 7 ft. 2 in. and is fitted with Tasker coupling. A 4-speed gearbox is employed and the brakes are hydraulically operated. Used by the RAF and Royal Navy for carrying aircraft, the SAG remained in production until 1957.

Example Preserved.

2128RN	Queen Mary	Royal Navy	Imperial War Museum, Duxford

BEDFORD SLG

Making its debut in 1951 the Bedford SLG was a 4 × 2 3-5-ton model of forward control layout. Having a wheelbase of 13 ft. 0 in., it was powered by a Bedford 6-cylinder petrol engine of 94 bhp. and had a 4-speed gearbox and hydraulic brakes. The SLG was used by both the RAF and the Army for aircraft servicing and for this purpose it was fitted with a Simon hydraulic platform. It continued in production until 1957.

Examples Preserved.

CVE525V   Servicing platform RAF   Imperial War Museum, Duxford

BLACK PRINCE

Designated Infantry Tank A43, the Black Prince was originally known as the 'Super Churchill'. This was no doubt due to the fact that the A43 used Churchill VII mechanical components as much as possible although much re-design work had been needed mainly because of the wider hull required. Six prototypes were built by Vauxhall early in 1945, but as hostilities in Europe had then ended, the A43 was not proceeded with and never entered production. Having a maximum speed of 11 mph., the Black Prince was fitted with Bedford Twin Six 350 hp. engines. Its main armament was 1 × 17 pdr. OQF whilst its secondary armament consisted of 2 × 7.92 cal. Besa MG, one of which was co-axial. It was 28 ft. 11 in. long, 11 ft. 3½ in. wide and 9 ft. 0 in. high.

Example Preserved.

1945   Tank   Brit. Army   RAC Museum, Bovington

BOARHOUND

Seen on display at the RAC Museum at Bovington is this 1944 Boarhound.

(K. A. Jenkinson)

Built in America by General Motors to British specifications, the Boarhound was an 8 × 8 heavy armoured car powered by 2 GMC 6-cylinder engines. Introduced in 1942, it was armed with 1 × 6 pdr. gun and 1 × .30 in. co-axial Browning MG. The steering, which could be power operated by selection, acted

26

on the front 4 wheels and the complete vehicle weighed 23.6 tons. It was discontinued in 1944.

Example Preserved.

1944	Armoured Car	Brit. Army	RAC Museum, Bovington

BUFFALO

This American built Buffalo tracked landing vehicle dating from 1943 is the only known example to be preserved.

(K. A. Jenkinson)

Officially termed LVT4, this American built tracked landing vehicle was used by the British army who christened it Buffalo. Being a hybrid amphibious tank it was capable of carring 30 troops and light vehicles (e.g. Jeeps) or field guns. Developed from the LVT(A)2, the LVT4 was powered by a Continental W-670 250 hp. engine and was first introduced in 1944. Troops and stores were loaded through the stern. The British army armed the Buffalo with 1 × Polsten 20 mm. cannon whilst in American service the LVT4 was equipped with a mount on each side for a .30 cal. or .50 cal. MG. It was 26 ft. 1 in. long, 10 ft. 1 in. wide and 8 ft. 1 in. high.

Example Preserved.

P346467	1943	LVT	Brit. Army	RAC Museum, Bovington

CARDEN-LOYD Mk.VI

Introduced towards the end of 1927, the Carden-Loyd Mk.VI machine gun carrier was built by Vickers-Armstrongs from 1928 after they acquired the patent rights of Carden and Loyd. Although based on the Mk.V, the Mk.VI did not have the tricycle wheel device. They were all delivered to the army devoid of mountings, and were then fitted out for the function they were to perform. Several variants of the Mk.VI were constructed including one with a completely covered head for the driver and gunner. Designed for a crew of 2, the Mk.VI was powered by a Ford model T 40 hp. engine and was armed with $1 \times .303$ Vickers MG. Being 8 ft. 1 in. long, 5 ft. 9 in. wide and 4 ft. 0 in. high, this excellent little machine gun carrier remained in production until 1930 by which time 270 had been built.

Example Preserved.

MT9909	1928	Gun Carrier	Brit. Army	RAC Museum, Bovington

CARRO ARMATO M13/40

This Carro Armato M13/40 tank, now preserved, was built in Italy for use by the British Army.
(K. A. Jenkinson)

The Italian built Carro Armato M13/40 medium tank went into production in 1940 powered by a SPA 8 TM40 8-cylinder diesel engine. Armed with 1×47 mm. gun, 1×8 mm. co-axial MG and 1×8 mm. MG (AA), with 2×8 mm. MG's in the front hull, it was 16 ft. 2 in. long, 7 ft. 3 in. wide and 7 ft. 10 in. high. In service it was found prone to breakdowns and was taken out of production in 1941.

Example Preserved.

3543	1940	Tank	Brit. Army	RAC Museum, Bovington

...nk T330553 was one built in 1944 for use by the British Army.

(K. A. Jenkinson)

...y built in pilot form as the T24 in October 1943, the Chaffee went into
...on during the spring of 1944 being re-designated Light Tank M24. The
...nufacturing plants of Cadillac and Massey-Harris undertook the pro-
...of the M24 which was armed with a 75 mm. M6 gun adapted from the
...craft cannon used in the Mitchell bomber. This had a concentric recoil
...which saved valuable turret space. Secondary armament consisted of
...l. Browning MG, one of which was co-axial, and 1 × .50 cal. AA MG.
...ffee was 18 ft. 0 in. long, 9 ft. 8 in. wide and 8 ft. 1½ in. high and was
...by Cadillac twin 44T24 petrol engines of 110 hp. each.

Preserved.

0553	1944	Tank	Brit. Army	RAC Museum, Bovington

CARRO VELOCE CV33

The Italian built Carro Veloce CV33 Tankette was produced by Fiat and first
appeared in 1933. Powered by a Fiat 4-cylinder petrol engine, it was armed with
twin 8 mm. Fiat MGs. Constructed to a length of 10 ft. 5 in. with a width of
4 ft. 7 in. and a height of 4 ft. 2 in., a number of variants were built for specific
purposes. Amongst these was the CV33 flamethrower. This more usually towed
a 2-wheeled trailer carrying 109 gallons of flame-fuel but in some cases, a tank
was mounted on the rear of the hull, this tank holding 13 gallons of the flame
fuel. The CV33 remained in production until 1938.

Example Preserved.

1840	1933	Tank	Italian Army	RAC Museum, Bovington

CENTAUR

Immaculately restored, Centaur tank T218477 looks as if it could still be called upon for use if the
occasion arose.

(P. Isaac)

Introduced in June 1942 as the second interim version of the heavy cruiser tank
to succeed the Crusader, the Centaur was first known as the Cromwell II.
Powered by a Nuffield Liberty 395 hp. engine it carried a crew of 5 and was
20 ft. 10 in. long, 9 ft. 6 in. wide and 8 ft. 2 in. high. The Centaur I was armed
with 1 × 6 pdr. and 1 or 2 Besa MG whilst the Centaur III had 1 × 75 mm. and 1
or 2 Besa MG and the Centaur IV had 1 × 95 mm. howitzer and 1 or 2 Besa MG.
The Centaur was built by Leyland Motors Ltd. and some were modified as anti-
aircraft tanks or as bulldozers. Production ended in 1945.

Examples Preserved.

T218477	1944	Tank	Brit. Army	Isaac, Umberleigh
	1944	Tank	Brit. Army	Marchant, Milton Keynes

CENTURION

Various types of Centurion tanks have been preserved, this one being a Bridgelayer dating from 1944.

(K. A. Jenkinson)

First appearing in 1945, the Centurion I was designated Cruiser Tank A41. Only 100 were built and all were powered by Rolls Royce Meteor V12 600 hp. engines. AEC were the production 'parents' for the Centurion and had it not been for the fact that hostilities had ceased before the first of this model had been delivered, it would have no doubt gone into full production. As it was however, the Centurion was modified resulting in the Mk.II appearing in prototype form later in 1945. So successful was the Centurion that it continued to be built and improved upon through 13 variants, the last of which were built in 1966 under Leyland parentage. The Centurion I was 25 ft. 2 in. long, 11 ft. 0 in. wide and 9 ft. 8 in. high and was mounted with 1 × 17 pdr. OQF together with 1 × 20 mm. Polsten cannon or 1 × Beas 7.92 cal. MG in turret front. The Centurion III was fitted with a Rolls Royce V12 650 hp. engine, 1 × 20 pdr. gun and 1 × Besa 7.92 cal. MG armament and was 32 ft. 3 in. long, 11 ft. 0¾ in. wide and 9 ft. 8 in. high whilst the Centurion XIII had the same engine as the Mk.III, was mounted with 1 × 105 mm. gun and 2 × 30 in. Browning 1-50 RG and was 32 ft. 4 in. long, 11 ft. 1½ in. wide and 9 ft. 10½ high. Another use to which the Centurion was put was as a bridgelayer, an example of which is now preserved.

Examples Preserved.

I	03ZR70	1945	Tank	Brit. Army	RAC Museum, Bovington
III	03ZR71	1959	Tank	Brit. Army	RAC Museum, Bovington
XIII	04CC87	1966	Tank	Brit. Army	RAC Museum, Bovington
Bridgelayer		1944	Bridgelayer	Brit. Army	RAC Museum, Bovington

CHAR B1-BIS

The Char B1-bis was a development of the Char B1, fi[...] Designated as a heavy tank, its hull was of cast secti[...] was powered by a Renault 6-cylinder petrol engine dev[...] 5 in. length, 8 ft. 2 in. width and 9 ft. 2 in. height, it w[...] gun with a very short barrel, and 1 × 7.5 mm. Chatelle[...] were in the hull and 1 × 37 mm. gun together with 1 × [...] the turret. Built for a crew of 4, the B1-bis remained in[...] of France in 1940.

Example Preserved.

1939　Tank　　　　　French Army [...]

CHAR SOMUA S-35

Char Somua S-35 67227 preserved at Bovington looks small at the side [...]

The French Char Somua S-35 was a medium tank built by [...] Ouen factory. Introduced in 1935, it was powered by [...] 8-cylinder petrol engine and was 17 ft. 11 in. long, 6 ft. [...] 10 in. high. Armed with 1 × 47 mm. gun and 1 × 7.5 mm. [...] was of three cast sections bolted together. It remained in pr[...]

Example Preserved.

67227　　　1935　Tank　　　　　French Army RAC [...]

CHAFF[...]

Chaffe[...]

Origi[...] prod[...] USA [...] ducti[...] heav[...] syste[...] 2 × [...] The [...] pow[...]

Exa[...]

CHARIOTEER

Built in the post-war era, Charioteer 04ZW12 was based on the Cromwell design but fitted with a new turret.

(K. A. Jenkinson)

The Charioteer was a British built tank destroyer developed in 1952. Powered by a Rolls Royce Meteor Mk.3 V12 petrol engine, it was basically a Cromwell fitted with a new turret and mounted with the same gun as used in the Centurion. It was 20 ft. 11 in. long, 10 ft. 1 in. wide and 9 ft. 1½ in. high and was armed with 1×84 mm. gun and 1×7.62 mm. coaxial MG. Six smoke dischargers were fitted to each side of the turret. The Charioteer continued to be built until 1954.

Example Preserved.

04ZW12   1953   Tank   Brit. Army   RAC Museum, Bovington

CHEVROLET C8

Fitted with a no.12 cab, this Chevrolet C8 is preserved in US Army colours.

(C. Pearce)

Appearing in 1940, the Chevrolet C8 was Canadian built, being a 4 × 2 model of semi-forward control layout. Given a wheelbase of 8 ft. 5 in., it has a Chevrolet 6-cylinder petrol engine of 85 bhp. whilst its gearbox is a 4-speed unit. Hydraulic brakes are fitted, acting on all wheels. Personnel/GS or wireless bodywork was fitted to this 8 cwt. model.

Examples Preserved.

	1940	Wireless House	Johns, Camberley
HAD133	1941		Worthing, Ludlow
	1941	Personnel	Sales, Surrey
		Personnel	Anderson, Newcastle
	1942	Personnel	Maddocks, Shrewsbury
		Personnel	Birnie, Herts
	1943	Personnel	Marchant, Milton Keynes

CHEVROLET C8A

Originally built for use by the Canadian Army, Chevrolet C8A JOR871L fitted with a no.13 cab is seen here at a rally.

(C. Pearce)

Introduced in 1942, the Chevrolet C8A was built by General Motors of Canada Ltd. It was an 8-cwt 4 × 4 heavy utility vehicle which could be fitted with a wide variety of bodywork including wireless, personnel carrier, ambulance, office or machinery set etc. It had a wheelbase of 8 ft. 5 in. and was powered by a Chevrolet 216-type 6-cylinder petrol engine. Transmission was via a 4-speed gearbox whilst its brakes were hydraulically operated acting on all 4-wheels. It remained in production until 1945 in which year it was re-designated 15-cwt 4 × 4.

Examples Preserved.

	1942	Wireless		Groom, Warlingham
JOR871L	1942		Brit. Army	Denton, Camberley
550CPC	1943	Ambulance	Can. Army	Vanderveen, Holland
HXU734	1944	Office	Can. Army	Museum, Los Angeles, USA
HUW830	1944	Wireless House Wireless	Can. Army	Warnham War Museum Coult, Harrow

CHEVROLET C15

The Chevrolet C15 was a 15 cwt 4×2 semi-forward control model built in Canada, India and Australia. Powered by a Chevrolet 216-type 6-cylinder petrol engine, it had a 4-speed gearbox and hydraulic brakes. Introduced in 1939 it had an 8 ft. 5 in. wheelbase and was used with various types of bodywork including general service, personnel, cable layer etc. The C15 saw service throughout the Commonwealth and remained in production until 1945.

Examples Preserved.

	1942	Chassis/Cab		Haylock, Maldon.
	1942	G/S Truck		Swift, Selby
DNL833	1942	G/S Truck	Brit. Army	Mankin, Heddon on the Wall
HUP310	1943	G/S Truck		Mankin, Heddon on the Wall
	1943	G/S Truck		Clifford, London
	1943	G/S Truck		Carmichael, Worcs.
	1943	G/S Truck		Jones, Shropshire
	1944	G/S Truck		Kennedy, Lancs

CHEVROLET C15A

KKO719L, a Chevrolet C15A fitted with a no.12 cab has been well restored to its original condition.
(C. Pearce)

Built in Canada and other Commonwealth countries, the Chevrolet C15A was a 15-cwt 4×4 model of semi-forward control layout. Having a wheelbase of 8 ft. 5 in. it was fitted with a Chevrolet 216-type 6-cylinder petrol engine and 4-speed gearbox whilst its brakes were of the hydraulic type acting on all 4 wheels. GS, van, office, wireless, cable layer, personnel or water tank bodywork was available and the C15A continued in production until 1945.

Examples Preserved.

BOY898H	1939	G/S Truck	Groom, Warlingham
BUX161	1941		Palmer, Cheltenham
	1941	G/S Truck	Mankin, Heddon on the Wall
	1941		N.W. Trans. Museum, Burtonwood
	1941	G/S Truck	Bayles, London
FOU658	1942	G/S Truck	Beddall, Iver
	1942	G/S Truck	Barnard, Newport, Essex
KKO719L	1944	G/S Truck	Priestley, Chelmsford

CHEVROLET C30

This preserved Chevrolet C30 4 × 4 vehicle is fitted with house-type bodywork.

(C. Pearce)

The Chevrolet C30 was a 30 cwt, 4 × 4 truck of semi-forward control layout built to Commonwealth design. Introduced in 1940, it had a wheelbase of 11 ft. 2 in. and was given a Chevrolet 6-cylinder petrol engine of 85 bhp. Transmission was via a 4-speed gearbox with 2-speed transfer box, the brakes being hydraulically operated. Various bodies were fitted to the C30 including office, light anti-aircraft tractor, GS, wireless etc. and the model continued in production until 1943.

Examples Preserved.

HKD133	1941	Wireless	Worthing, Orleton
	1941	G/S Truck	Broom, Somerset
GUY 161	1942	Signals Van	Mansell, Pershore

CHEVROLET C60

The British Commonwealth built Chevrolet C60 was a 3-ton 4 × 4 truck of semi-forward control layout. Given a choice of 11 ft. 2 in. or 13 ft. 2 in. wheelbase (classified C60S and C60L respectively), the model was first built in 1940 and was powered by a Chevrolet 85 bhp. 6-cylinder petrol engine. Transmission was via a 4-speed gearbox with 2-speed transfer and the brakes were hydraulically operated. A wide range of bodywork was used including GS, stores, dental, machinery, office, petrol tanker, wrecker, wireless, dump and derrick etc. The C60 remained in production until 1945.

Examples Preserved.

C60S	LA0532	1942	Recovery Truck	Mankin, Heddon on the Wall
C60L		1942	Recovery Truck	Wilson, Hexham

CHEVROLET CGT

Introduced in 1940, the Chevrolet CGT was a 30 cwt 4 × 4 vehicle of semi-forward control layout. Having a wheelbase of 8 ft. 5 in. it used a Chevrolet 6-cylinder 85 bhp. petrol engine, 4-speed gearbox with 2-speed transfer and hydraulic brakes. The CGT was used as an AT Portee, and a field artillery tractor and it continued to be built until 1945.

Examples Preserved.

UPO636K	1941	Artillery Tractor	Brit. Army	Belsey, Storrington
OPG312R	1944	Artillery Tractor		Wandsworth, Hurtmore

CHEVROLET K43

Chevrolet K43 PGC123 is seen here after its initial rebuild to driving order. This rare vehicle is again being rebuilt to achieve its complete authenticity.

(G. W. T. McMillan)

The Chevrolet K43 of the G-7100 series was introduced in 1942 as a 4×4 1½-ton model. Having a wheelbase of 12 ft. 1 in. it was powered by a Chevrolet 6-cylinder petrol engine of 235.5 cu. in. and had a 4-speed gearbox with 2-speed transfer box and hydraulic (Hydrovac) brakes. The K43 carried telephone maintenance bodywork with winch for use by the Signal Corps. It remained in production until 1945.

Example Preserved.

PGC123   1943   Telephone Truck   McMillan, Falkirk

CHEVROLET YP-G-4112

Built in 1940, this Chevrolet YP-G tipper MPK112 originally served with the US Army.

(R. F. Mack)

Introduced in 1940, the Chevrolet YP-G-4112 was a 1½ ton 4×4 normal control model with a wheelbase of 12 ft. 1 in. Powered by a Chevrolet 93 bhp. 6-cylinder petrol engine it had a 4-speed gearbox with 2-speed transfer box and was fitted with hydrovac brakes. A number of different bodies could be specified including tipper, cargo, van, tipper and oil service. The YP-G-4112 remained in production until 1941.

Examples Preserved.

MPK112	1940	Tipper	US Army	Warnham War Museum
	1941	G/S Truck		Robinson & Webb, Duxford
	1941	G/S Truck		Chapman, Kettering

CHIEFTAIN

Comparatively new in the preservation field, Chieftain tank 01DC87 was built in 1962.

(K. A. Jenkinson)

Based on a design evolved in 1959, the Chieftain is regarded as a main battle tank. Built at the ROF, Leeds and at Vickers Elswick works, a small number of prototypes were built between 1959 and 1962, full production not being started until 1967. Powered by a Leyland L60 multi-fuel 6-cylinder engine with 12 vertically opposed pistons, the Chieftain is 24 ft. 8 in. long, 12 ft. 0 in. wide and 9 ft. 6 in. high. It is armed with 1 × 120 mm. gun, 2 × 7.62 mm. MG (one of which is co-axial), 1 × .5 in. MG and 12 smoke dischargers (6 on each side of the turret). As well as being built as a main battle tank, the Chieftain has also been built as an armoured recovery vehicle and a bridgelayer. In 1971 a new version designated the Shir Iran was introduced, fitted with a Rolls Royce 12-cylinder diesel engine, and this variant is still being produced for service in Kuwait.
The Chieftain was preceded by a tank known as the FV4202. This was designed by Leyland using some Centurion components and two were built for test purposes in 1956/7. No further FV4202's were built.

Examples Preserved.

01DC87	1962	Tank	Brit. Army	RAC Museum, Bovington

CHURCHILL

Various marques of Churchill tanks have been preserved, T347848M being a Churchill VIII dating from 1945.

(K. A. Jenkinson)

Following four prototypes built by Harland & Wolff Ltd., Belfast in 1940, Vauxhall Motors Ltd. were asked to design and produce the Churchill infantry tank as the successor to the Matilda. The first prototype from Luton was tested by the end of 1940 and the first production models were in service by June 1941. Built as an infantry tank, the Churchill proved extremely reliable and as time went on, it was improved in armament as well as in numerous other ways. Powered by a Bedford Twin-Six petrol engine of 350 hp. made up of two 6-cylinder Bedford truck engines, the Churchill was 24 ft. 5 in. long, 9 ft. 0 in. wide and 10 ft. 8 in. (11 ft. 4 in. Mks. VII-VIII) high. It was built by a production group consisting of Broom & Wade, Birmingham Carriage & Wagon Co., Metropolitan Cammell, Charles Roberts, Newton Chambers, Gloucester Railway Carriage, Leyland, Dennis and Harland & Wolff, all under the 'parentage' of Vauxhall. Amongst the numerous marques built was the Churchill VI, introduced in 1943. This was mounted with a 75 mm. gun developed by Vickers and was really a Mk.IV brought up to Mk.VII standards. During the following year, the Churchill VII made its appearance. This was given heavier integral armour, heavier suspension, a new cast/welded turret with cupola, circular escape doors and a number of other refinements. Other Churchill variants were also built in smaller numbers and these included a Flail, a Bridgelayer, Ark and AVRE (Armoured Vehicle, Royal Engineers) models. It was not until 1951 that production of the Churchill finally ceased.

Examples Preserved.

IV		1950	Ark	Brit. Army	RAC Museum, Bovington
VI		1942	Tank	Brit. Army	RAC Museum, Bovington
VII	T347848M	1945	Tank	Brit. Army	RAC Museum, Bovington
VII		1948	Bridgelayer	Brit. Army	RAC Museum, Bovington
VII	251892		Crocodile	Brit. Army	Isaac, Umberleigh

CITROEN-KEGRESSE

Development of the Citroen-Kegresse dates back to 1921 when the prototype was constructed. Being a half-track car using Kegresse-Hinstin bogies on a Citroen 10CV car chassis, the model was gradually updated and modified until World War II. During its course of production, both 4 and 6-cylinder petrol engines were used and two gear levers were fitted—one for the 4-speed main gearbox, the other for the 2-speed transfer box. A variety of bodywork was fitted including some which were armoured and the Citroen-Kegresse fulfilled numerous duties and roles during its production life.

Examples Preserved.

	1928		French Army	Oliver, Eton, Wick
BPU875	1928	Staff Car		Black, Keighley

CLETRAC

Now preserved at Duxford is this Cletrac tractor.

(D. Game)

Introduced in 1941, the Clectrac M2 7-ton high speed tractor was built in the USA by the Cleveland Tractor Co. Being a fully tracked vehicle it was almost exclusively used by the air forces for aircraft towing and it was used in Britain by the RAF. It was powered by a Hercules 6-cylinder 137 bhp. petrol engine and used a 4-speed gearbox. An auxiliary generator was driven from the front PTO., whilst a rear-mounted compressor was driven by the main engine. It carried a crew of three and the Cletrac remained in production until 1945.

Examples Preserved.

1942	Tractor	USAF	Imperial War Museum, Duxford.
1943	Tractor		Marchant, Milton Keynes

COMET I

One of two Comet I's to be preserved, 09ZR88 was built in 1945.

(K. A. Jenkinson)

The Comet I, this being the name given to the Cruiser Tank A34, was of all welded construction and could be distinguished from the Cromwell by having return rollers above its road wheels. Developed by Leyland from the Cromwell design, production of the Comet I began in 1944 and was fitted with a new compact version of the Vickers-Armstrong 17 pdr. gun. This was of lighter weight than the previous 17 pdr. and had a shorter barrel and shorter breech. In addition to this, the Comet I was given secondary armament of 2 × Besa 7.92 cal. MG, one of which was co-axial. Being of 25 ft. 1½ in. length, 8 ft. 9½ in. height and 10 ft. 0 in. width, the Comet proved a fast and reliable tank. Production continued into 1945 and some remained in service until the early 1960s. The power unit fitted to the Comet I was a Rolls Royce V12 600 hp. engine.

Examples Preserved.

09ZR88	1945	Tank	Brit. Army	RAC Museum, Bovington
	1945		Brit. Army	Imperial War Museum, Duxford

COMMER Q2

The Commer Q2 was a 15 cwt. 4×2 semi-forward control vehicle with a wheelbase of 10 ft. 0 in. Introduced in 1939 it was powered by a Commer 6-cylinder petrol engine rated at 20.92 hp. and had a 4-speed crash gearbox and hydraulically operated brakes. In 1942 its original engine was superceded by a Commer 6-cylinder 27 hp. petrol engine. It could be fitted with various types of bodywork and was also available with a longer, 12 ft. 9 in. wheelbase. It remained in production until 1948. In addition to this model, the Commer Q2 was also built as a forward control tractor unit for coupling to a semi-trailer of 40 ft. 0 in. length, known as a 'Queen Mary' for use by the RAF. In this form it had a wheelbase of 8 ft. 0 in. and its brakes were given servo assistance.

Examples Preserved.

ZD3428	1943	Tractor	TMS, Castleruddery
CPR104	1943	Tractor	Barnard, Seaton

CONQUEROR

The Conqueror heavy tank was put into production in 1956 after some prototypes built earlier had been thoroughly tested. Equipped with 1×120 mm. gun, 1×.3 in. co-axial MG, 1×.3 in. MG on the commander's cupola and 6 smoke dischargers on each side of the turret, the Conqueror is 25 ft. 4 in. long, 13 ft. 1 in. wide and 11 ft. 0 in. high. It is powered by a Rolls Royce Meteor 12-cylinder petrol engine and has a maximum armour of 178 mm. A total of 180 Conquerors were built before production ended in 1959.

Examples Preserved.

40BA86	1952	Tank	Brit. Army	RAC Museum, Bovington
05BA94			Brit. Army	Imperial War Museum, Duxford.

COVENTRY Mk.I

Produced as a combined effort between Humber, Commer and Daimler, the Coventry armoured car used a design co-ordinated by Humber, who also undertook the detail work connected with the hull, turret, armament and engine. Commer were responsible for the design of the axles, gearbox and transmission whilst Daimler undertook responsibility for the steering and suspension. The first Coventry armoured car prototype was completed in 1944 and after this, the Coventry went into full production at the Rootes Group and Daimler factories. It was a 4×4 vehicle powered by a Hercules RXLD-type 6-cylinder 175 bhp. petrol engine with 5 forward and 5 reverse gears. It had a wheelbase of 9 ft. 10 in. and was 15 ft. 6½ in. long, 8 ft. 9 in. wide and 7 ft. 9 in. high. Carrying a crew of 4 it was armed with 1×2 pdr. gun and 1×co-axial Besa MG. Few had been built however when production ceased in 1945.

Example Preserved.

	1944	Armoured Car	Brit. Army	RAC Museum, Bovington

CROMWELL IV

T190003, a Cromwell IV of 1942 vintage is safely preserved at the RAC Museum, Bovington.
(K. A. Jenkinson)

The Cruiser tank Mk. VIII A27M as the Cromwell was designated was basically a modified Crusader fitted with a Meteor engine. Birmingham Carriage & Wagon Co. delivered the first mild steel prototype on 1st March 1942 and general production started in January 1943, by which time Leyland had become the design and production 'parent' for the entire A27 series. The Cromwell IV was really a Centaur III re-engined with a Rolls Royce Meteor V12 600 hp. engine to bring it to A27 standards. Armament was provided by 1×75 mm. gun and $2 \times$ Besa 7.92 cal. MG, and the Cromwell IV was 20 ft. 10 in. long, 9 ft. 6½ in. wide and 8 ft. 2 in. high. Being numerically the most important British-built cruiser tank of World War II, the Cromwell remained in production until 1945.

Example Preserved.

T190003	1942	Tank	Brit. Army	RAC Museum, Bovington

CROSSLEY 6×4 ARMOURED

The only known surviving Crossley 6×4 armoured AA car is this example which can be seen at Bovington.

(K. A. Jenkinson)

Introduced in 1928, the Crossley 6×4 armoured anti-aircraft car was powered by a 4-cylinder 26 hp. petrol engine and had a 4-speed gearbox with 2-speed transfer box. Its original turret was later replaced by twin Vickers 50 in. machine guns and the armoured bodywork was built by Vickers. The model remained in production until 1931.

Example Preserved.

1930	Armoured AA Car Brit. Army	RAC Museum, Bovington

CROSSLEY IGL8

Introduced in 1935, the Crossley IGL8 was a forward control 3 ton 6×4 vehicle with a wheelbase of 12 ft. 10 in. Powered by a Crossley 4-cylinder petrol engine of 5266 cc., it had a 4-speed gearbox with 2-speed transfer box and servo assisted mechanically operated brakes. Various types of bodywork could be fitted including GS, breakdown, workshop, searchlight, derrick and Coles crane. The IGL8 remained in production until 1941.

Example Preserved.

KUJ138	1939	Breakdown	Seabury, Shrewsbury

CROSSLEY Q2

The Crossley Q2 made its debut in April 1940 and was built solely for the RAF. A forward control 3-tonner of 4 × 4 configuration, it had a wheelbase of 11 ft. 6 in. and was powered by a Crossley 4-cylinder petrol engine of 96 bhp. Transmission was via a 4-speed gearbox with 2-speed transfer box and the Q2 was given GS, workshop, fire tender and MT breakdown bodywork. It remained in production until 1944.

Example Preserved.

Chassis/cab	RAF	Webb & Seabrook, Baldock

CROSSLEY-TASKER

Intoduced in October 1943, the Crossley-Tasker unit consisted of a Crossley 4 × 4, 5-ton tractor unit and a Tasker 'Queen Mary' semi-trailer, the complete unit having an overall length of 50 ft. The tractor unit was of forward control layout with a wheelbase of 8 ft. 5¾ in. and was powered by a Crossley 4-cylinder engine of 91 bhp. It had a 4-speed gearbox with a 2-speed transfer box and hydraulic brakes, these being servo assisted. A 2-ton collapsible ballast body was fitted behind the cab for use when towing full-trailers. Built for the RAF, it remained in production until 1944.

Examples Preserved.

Queen Mary	RAF	Rowell, Peterborough
Queen Mary	RAF	Lambe, Fenstanton

CRUISER TANK Mk.I & Mk.II

The Cruiser tank was comparatively small in size as can be seen from T9261, a Mk.II of 1938 vintage.

(K. A. Jenkinson)

Designed by Sir John Carden in 1934, the Cruiser Tank Mk.I, designated the A9 was to be a new medium tank incorporating the best features of the discontinued Medium Mk.III, but being much lighter in weight. Production commenced in 1937, the pilot model having been built a year earlier. Of the 125 built, 50 were constructed by Vickers with the remaining 75 coming from Harland & Wolff, Belfast. Armament consisted of 1 × 2 pdr. OQF and 3 × Vickers .303 cal. MG (one co-axial). It had a length of 19 ft. 0 in. height of 8 ft. 8½ in. and width of 8 ft. 2½ in. and was powered by an AEC 6-cylinder A179-type petrol engine of 150 hp. In service, the A9 proved to have too slow a speed for the 'cruiser' role and had inadequate armour and thus saw little service after 1941.

The Cruiser Tank Mk.II, of which the pilot was completed in July 1937 was basically a more heavily armoured A9 and used the same basic boat-shaped hull etc. Designated A10, the Mk.II achieved its additional armour by simply bolting additional plates on to the outside of the hull and turret, whilst the auxiliary machine gun turrets were discarded. Its engine was the same as that of the A9, its armament being 1 × 2 pdr. QFSA and 2 × Besa MG. Production commenced in 1938 and was completed by September 1940 with 10 being built by Vickers, 45 by Metropolitan Cammell and 120 by Birmingham Railway Carriage & Wagon Co.

Examples Preserved.

I	PMV586	1938	Tank	Brit. Army	RAC Museum, Bovington
II	T9261	1938		Brit. Army	RAC Museum, Bovington

CRUISER TANK Mk.III

Built a year later was this Cruiser Mk.III tank, used originally by the British Army.

(K. A. Jenkinson)

The Cruiser tank Mk.III, designated the A13 was an important step in the development of British tanks, being fitted with Christie suspension. Its conception stemmed from the designs developed by the American designer J. Walter Christie. Nuffields built the prototype A13 during 1937 and fitted it with a Nuffield Liberty V12 340 hp. engine. Full production began in 1938 by Nuffield Mechanisations & Aero Ltd., a company formed specially for munitions work by Morris, and the first A13 rolled off the assembly line early in 1939. Some 65 were built, the last of which was completed by the summer of 1939. A 1 × 2 pdr. QFSA and 1 × Vickers .303 cal. MG were employed whilst the dimensions of the A13 were 19 ft. 9 in. long, 8 ft. 4 in. wide and 8 ft. 6 in. high.

Example Preserved.

1939	Tank	Brit. Army	RAC Museum, Bovington

CRUSADER III

Shown here with camouflage markings, is a preserved 1942 Crusader III.

(K. A. Jenkinson)

The final production version of the Crusader A15 Mk.VI Cruiser tank, the Crusader III was first tested in prototype form in December 1941. Nuffields acted as the 'parent' company to a group of nine companies engaged in production of the A15 range and all used the Nuffield Liberty V12 340 hp. engine. The total number of Crusader A15s built was 5,300, of which 144 were Crusader IIIs. These were built in the short space of time between May and July 1942 and were 19 ft. 8 in. long, 8 ft. 8 in. wide and 7 ft. 4 in. high. Armament given was 1 × 6 pdr. OQF and 1 or 2 × Besa 7.92 cal. MG. A riveted hull and welded turret was used with an outer layer of armour bolted on.

Example Preserved.

1942	Tank		Brit. Army	RAC Museum, Bovington

DAIMLER Mk.I ARMOURED CAR

Looking like an enlarged scout car, the Daimler Armoured Car went into production in 1941.
(K. A. Jenkinson)

The Daimler Armoured Car first entered service in 1941, and in appearance was an enlarged version of the Daimler Scout Car. It had no chassis, all the running gear being attached to strongpoints in the hull. Its rear mounted engine was a Daimler 6-cylinder petrol unit with fluid flywheel, 5-speed pre-selector gearbox and transfer box. Being a 4×4 model, it carried 1×2 pdr. gun and 1×7.92 mm. Besa co-axial MG for armament. The Mk.I was superceded in 1943 by the Mk.II which differed mainly in the type of gun mounting, drivers escape hatch and engine covers. Around 2,700 were built before production stopped in 1944.

Examples Preserved.

37ZU35	1941	Armoured Car	Brit. Army	RAC Museum, Bovington
F209485	1942	Armoured Car	Brit. Army	Imperial War Museum, Duxford
	1942	Armoured Car	Brit. Army	Wilkinson, St. Albans
	1942	Armoured Car	Brit. Army	Marchant, Milton Keynes
	1943	Armoured Car	Brit. Army	McIntrye, Sorn Castle

DAIMLER SCOUT CAR

Introduced in 1940, the Daimler Mk.I scout car—often referred to as the Dingo—used a 4×4 configuration to give it good cross-country mobility. Powered by a Daimler 2.52 litre 6-cylinder petrol engine, it had a 6 ft. 6 in. wheelbase, 5-speed pre-selector gearbox and transfer box. 4-wheel steering was provided on the Mk.I, but the Mk.II introduced in 1941 dispensed with this. It was armed with 1×.303 cal. Besa LMG. Hydraulic brakes were fitted, these acting on all 4 wheels. The Mk.II also differed from the Mk.I by having different radiator grilles whilst the Mk.III which first appeared in 1943 had no overhead armour. 6,626 Daimler Scout Cars were built before production ended at the end of 1944.

Examples Preserved.

	1941	Scout Car	Brit. Army	Pearce, Holywell
AJW420H	1942	Scout Car	Brit. Army	Beddall, Iver
GPE797J	1942	Scout Car	Brit. Army	Mutch, Aberlady
LGF458P	1942	Scout Car	Brit. Army	MT Pres. Group, Croydon
YPO90G	1942	Scout Car	Brit. Army	Warnham War Museum
	1942	Scout Car	Brit. Army	Langley, Highwich
	1942	Scout Car	Brit. Army	McIntyre, Ayrshire
	1942	Scout Car	Brit. Army	Isaac, Barnstaple
	1942	Scout Car	Brit. Army	Wilkinson, St. Albans
	1942	Scout Car	Brit. Army	Spickernell, Salop
	1942	Scout Car	Brit. Army	Robinson, Burton Latimer
	1942	Scout Car	Brit. Army	West, Surrey
	1942	Scout Car	Brit. Army	Gill, Yeovil
	1942	Scout Car	Brit. Army	James, Malvern
	1942	Scout Car	Brit. Army	Hickman, Worcs.
	1942	Scout Car	Brit. Army	Mann, Lamanva
	1943	Scout Car	Brit. Army	Thompson, Alnwick
195FUF	1943	Scout Car	Brit. Army	Mitchell, Upper Hartfield
	1943	Scout Car	Brit. Army	Mills, Barnstaple
F117637	1943	Scout Car	Brit. Army	Imperial War Museum, Duxford
KPH271K	1943	Scout Car	Brit. Army	Groom, Warlingham
KTU97N	1943	Scout Car	Brit. Army	Houlahan & Busby, Hook Norton
OPN177M	1943	Scout Car	Brit. Army	Warnham War Museum
	1943	Scout Car	Brit. Army	RAC Museum, Bovington
	1943	Scout Car	Brit. Army	Bouts, Wolverhampton
	1943	Scout Car	Brit. Army	Mayer, Cheshunt
	1943	Scout Car	Brit. Army	Blyth, Holt
	1943	Scout Car	Brit. Army	Eagle, Essex
	1943	Scout Car	Brit. Army	Marchant, Milton Keynes
	1943	Scout Car	Brit. Army	Miller, Lincs.
	1943	Scout Car	Brit. Army	Guy, Ringwood
321DEL	1944	Scout Car	Brit. Army	Chidley, Taunton
VPF398G	1944	Scout Car	Brit. Army	Johns, Camberley
	1944	Scout Car	Brit. Army	Honeychurch, Salop
CNL138V	1944	Scout Car	Brit. Army	Anderson, Otterburn
	1944	Scout Car	Brit. Army	Mann, Lamanva
	1944	Scout Car	Brit. Army	Barn, Newport
JBP582H	1945	Scout Car	Brit. Army	Batterick, Lancing
	1945	Scout Car	Brit. Army	Smith, Bournemouth

DAVID BROWN TASKMASTER

Used as an aircraft tractor, this David Brown Taskmaster is seen here awaiting preservation.

(P. Isaac)

Introduced in 1941 the David Brown Taskmaster was an aircraft towing tractor with a wheelbase of 7 ft. 3 in. Powered by a 4-cylinder diesel engine 36 bhp., it had a dry twin plate clutch and torque converter and was available with a 4-speed gearbox on the Mk.I and Mk.II models or a 6-speed gearbox on the Mk.III. Capable of towing aircraft of up to 60,000 lbs. it remained in production until 1948.

Examples Preserved.

RGX25G	1942	Aircraft towing tractor RAF	Imperial War Museum, Duxford
	1944	Aircraft towing tractor RAF	Clements, Kings Nympton
	1944	Aircraft towing tractor RAF	Duxford Aviation Society

DENNIS MAX Mk.II

Built for use by the RAF, VP0558 is a beautifully restored example of the Dennis Max Mk.II.
(K. A. Jenkinson collection)

Introduced in June 1944, the Dennis Max Mk.II was a 6-ton 4 × 2 GS lorry of forward control layout. Having a wheelbase of 14 ft. 0 in. it was powered by a Dennis 04 type 4-cylinder diesel engine of 6.5 litres capacity and had a 5-speed gearbox with overdrive top. Hydraulically operated vacuum servo assisted brakes acted on all 4 wheels. The cab was fitted with a 3-piece windscreen and the Max Mk.II was used mainly by the RAF. It remained in production until 1945.

Example Preserved.

VP0558	1944	Searchlight Carrier RAF	Stanbridge, Cowfold

DENNIS 3-TON

The only preserved example of the Dennis 3-ton lorry is 401FAA, seen here after civilian use before restoration had commenced.

Being a civilian vehicle adapted for military use, the Dennis 3-ton 4×2 introduced in 1939 was a semi-forward control model with a wheelbase of 9 ft. 8 in. Powered by a Dennis 4-cylinder petrol of 75 bhp., it had a 4-speed gearbox and hydraulic brakes. End tipper dropside bodywork was most usually fitted (using Edbro hydraulic gear) and the Dennis 3-ton remained in production throughout the war years.

Example Preserved.

401FAA	1942	Tipper		Brit. Army	Crook, Melksham

DIAMOND T 968A

Fitted with troop carrier bodywork, PPX594K is a Diamond T968A built in 1945.

(C. Pearce)

Making its debut in 1941, the Diamond T 968A is a normal control 6×6 4-ton model of American origin, widely used in all the theatres of war and supplied to other nations under the Lend-Lease scheme. Given a wheelbase of 12 ft. 7 in. it is powered by a Hercules RXC 6-cylinder engine of 106 bhp. and has a 5-speed gearbox with overdrive top and 2-speed transfer box. Air brakes are fitted and the 968A was available with most types of bodywork including cargo and wrecker. It remained in production until 1945.

Examples Preserved.

	1943	G/S Truck		Bowman, Blaydon
	1943	Wrecker	US Army	Mann, Lamanva
PPX594K	1945	Troop Carrier	US Army	Gray, Worthing

DIAMOND T 969

Authentically restored as an American heavy wrecker, this is a Diamond T969A.

(K. A. Jenkinson)

Entering production in 1941, the Diamond T 969 was a 4-ton 6×6 model of normal control layout. Powered by a Hercules RXC 6-cylinder petrol engine of 106 bhp., it had a 5-speed gearbox with 2-speed transfer box and full air brakes. Used as a heavy wrecker, the 969 had a wheelbase of 12 ft. 7 in. and continued in production until 1945.

Examples Preserved.

1942	Wrecker		Wallsgrove, Warwicks.
1943	Wrecker	US Army	Mann, Lamanva

DIAMOND T 972

Introduced in 1941, the 4-ton 6×6 Diamond T 972 had a wheelbase of 12 ft. 7 in. and was of normal control layout. Fitted with a Hercules RXC 106 bhp. 6-cylinder petrol engine and 5-speed gearbox with 2-speed transfer, it had air brakes. Dump type bodywork was fitted and the 972 continued to be built until 1945.

Example Preserved.

1942	Dump Truck		Taverner, Cardiff

DIAMOND T 980

First produced in 1941, the Diamond T 980 was a 12-ton 6 × 4 Prime Mover of normal control layout with a wheelbase of 14 ft. 11¼ in. Powered by a Hercules DFXE type 6-cylinder diesel engine of 185 bhp., it had a 4-speed gearbox and 3-speed transfer box and air brakes. The 980 had a 300 ft. winch cable and 2 winch-cable roller sheaves at the rear. It was originally designed to meet a British requirement and first went into action with the British Army in North Africa. It was later also used by the US Army. It had a ballast body behind the cab and was used mainly for the recovery and transport of damaged tanks. It remained in production until 1945.

Example Preserved.

	1943	Prime Mover		Brit. Army	Bowman, Blaydon

DIAMOND T 981

GGF814, a Diamond T981 tank transporter shows its size at an HCVC London-Brighton Run.
(C. Pearce)

The Diamond T 981 was placed in service in 1941. Built as a tank transporter it was a 6 × 4 tractor of normal control layout. Its engine was a Hercules DFXE-type 6-cylinder diesel unit with a bore and stroke of 5⅝ in. × 6 in. whilst transmission was via a 4-speed gearbox to a double reduction spiral bevel rear axle. Full air brakes were fitted and the 981 had a wheelbase of 14 ft. 11¼ in. The 981 was also fitted with a winch, and it remained in production until the summer of 1945.

Examples Preserved.

	1942	Prime Mover		Brown, Bristol
302FAM	1943	Tank Transporter	US Army	Bishop, Yardley
GGF814	1944	Tank Transporter	Brit. Army	Stanier, Gravesend
ARG870V	1944	Tank Transporter	Brit. Army	Bowman, Blaydon

DODGE D15

The Dodge D15 typifies the numerous trucks adapted for military use based on civilian models.

(K. A. Jenkinson)

The British Commonwealth built Dodge D15 was a 4 × 2 normal control 15 cwt. 4 × 2 vehicle. Having a wheelbase of 10 ft. 8½ in., it was powered by a Dodge 6-cylinder 95 bhp. petrol engine and had a 4-speed gearbox and hydraulic brakes. Its most common use was as a GS truck or as a water tanker. Introduced in 1940, it remained in production until 1945.

Examples Preserved.

JKB880	1943	Cargo Truck	Brit. Army	Mankin, Heddon on the Wall
	1943	Desert Truck	Brit. Army	Groombridge, Heathfield
FUF52	1944	Breakdown	Brit. Army	Warnham War Museum
	1944	Cargo Truck		Hamilton, Old Plean

DODGE WC3

With its canvas tilt in position is GTX241N, a Dodge WC3 bearing American markings.

(C. Pearce)

The Dodge WC3 was a ½-ton 4×4 model of normal control layout first introduced in 1941. Having a 9 ft. 8 in. wheelbase, the WC3 was originally fitted with a Dodge T207 6-cylinder engine of 85 bhp., but from late 1941 a T215 92 bhp. 6-cylinder engine was used. Transmission was via a 4-speed gearbox and the brakes were of the hydraulic type. Built with Weapons Carrier bodywork, 7,808 WC3's were built before the model was discontinued in 1942.

Examples Preserved.

	1941	Weapons Carrier	US Army	Chapman, Kettering
GTX241N	1941	Weapons Carrier	US Army	Private Owner

DODGE WC6

753LPG is a Dodge WC6—a type which saw use during the Second World War.

(C. Pearce)

Introduced in 1941, the ½-ton 4 × 4 Dodge WC6 with its normal control layout had a wheelbase of 9 ft. 8 in. Powered by a Dodge T207 85 bhp. 6-cylinder petrol engine it had a 4-speed gearbox and hydraulic brakes. Command Reconnaissance bodywork was fitted and the WC6 of which 9,365 were built continued in production until 1942.

Examples Preserved.

CJR135	1941	Reconnaissance	US Army	Ashton, Sedgefield
	1941	Reconnaissance	US Army	Chapman, Kettering
	1941	Reconnaissance	US Army	Taverner, Cardiff
GPK67K	1942	Reconnaissance	US Army	Groombridge, Heathfield
	1942	Reconnaissance	US Army	Phelps, Glos.
753LPG	1942	Reconnaissance	US Army	Reynolds, London
SNX824M	1942	Reconnaissance	US Army	Fortnum, Rugby

DODGE WC7

Dodge WC7 WKL345J closely resembles the WC6 model other than its being fitted with a winch.
(K. A. Jenkinson collection)

Using a Dodge T207 chassis, the WC7 is a 4×4 US built vehicle of normal control layout of the ½-ton type. Introduced in 1941, it is powered by a Dodge 92 bhp. 6-cylinder petrol engine and has a wheelbase of 9 ft. 8 in. A 4-speed gearbox is used and the brakes which act on all four wheels are hydraulically operated. Command Reconnaissance bodywork with winch is fitted, and the WC7 remained in production until 1942, with a total of 1,438 having been built.

Example Preserved.

WKL345J 1941 Command Car. US Army Lamb, Sevenoaks

DODGE WC8

Making its debut in 1941, the WC8 was a ½-ton 4×4 vehicle of normal control layout and had a wheelbase of 9 ft. 8 in. It was powered by a Dodge 6-cylinder petrol engine of 85 bhp. and had a 4-speed gearbox and hydraulic brakes. The WC8 although closely resembling the WC6 in appearance was in fact fitted with radio equipment. The WC8 remained in production until 1942.

Example Preserved.

29836 1941 Radio US Army Warnham War Museum

DODGE WC42

The Dodge WC42 was introduced in 1941. A ½-ton 4×4 model of normal control layout it had a wheelbase of 9 ft. 8 in. and was powered by a Dodge T215 92 bhp. 6-cylinder petrol engine. Transmission was via a 4-speed gearbox whilst the brakes were hydraulically operated. Only 650 WC42's were built, all of which had Panel Radio bodywork and the last was completed in 1942.

Example Preserved.

1941	Radio Van	US Army	Marchant, Milton Keynes

DODGE WC51

Dodge WC51 weapons-carrier CDG847 stands on display at the Warnham War Museum.

(K. A. Jenkinson)

Using a Dodge T214 type 4×4 ¾-ton chassis, the WC51 was built in the US Given a wheelbase of 8 ft. 2 in., and of normal control layout, it is powered by a Dodge 6-cylinder petrol engine of 92 bhp. with a bore of 3¼ in. and a stroke of 4⅝ in. Transmission is via a 4-speed gearbox and its hydraulic brakes operate on all four wheels. Introduced in 1942, the WC51 is fitted with Weapons Carrier bodywork and it was also produced in Canada by Chrysler. The WC51 was used by the British Army (Lend-Lease) during World War II and it remained in production until 1945.

Examples Preserved.

DUY145	1942	Weapons Carrier		James, Evesham
JPO153J	1942	Weapons Carrier	USAF	Warnham War Museum
CDG847	1943	Weapons Carrier	US Army	Warnham War Museum

	1943	Weapons Carrier	US Army	Orpin, Oxon
	1943	Weapons Carrier		Millman, Devon
	1943	Weapons Carrier		Johnson, Kent
	1943	Weapons Carrier		Worthing, Ludlow
ULX993	1943	Weapons Carrier		Payne, Hest Bank
RMX335R	1943	Weapons Carrier	Brit. Army	Hamilton, Old Plean
	1943	Weapons Carrier		Jones, Salop
GTX291N	1943	Weapons Carrier	US Army	Dear, Brighton
PRW738W	1944	Weapons Carrier		Collen, Leamington Spa
	1944	Weapons Carrier		McIntyre, Sorn Castle

DODGE WC52

JKN589, ex US Army is a Dodge WC52 weapons carrier with winch.

(K. A. Jenkinson)

Introduced in 1942, the Dodge WC52 was built in the US as a 4×4 of normal control layout based on a Dodge T214 chassis. This ¾-ton model has a wheelbase of 8 ft. 2 in. and is powered by a Dodge 6-cylinder petrol engine of 92 bhp. Transmission is via a 4-speed gearbox with single speed transfer box, whilst the brakes act on all four wheels and are hydraulically operated. The bodywork used was as a weapons carrier with winch, and the WC52 remained in production until 1945. It was also built in Canada and fitted with truck bodywork. The WC52 saw service with the British Army (Lend-Lease) during the war.

Examples Preserved.

CBW7	1942	Weapons Carrier		Groom, Warlingham
JKN589	1943	Weapons Carrier	US Army	Groombridge, Heathfield
	1943	Weapons Carrier		Le Gresley, Jersey
	1943	Weapons Carrier		Page, Norwich
	1943	Weapons Carrier		Phelps, Glos.
	1944	Weapons Carrier		Murray, Belfast
	1944	Weapons Carrier		Mann, Lamanva
	1944	Weapons Carrier		Oakford, Princes Risborough
	1944	Weapons Carrier		Clifford, London
SYG57	1945	Weapons Carrier	US Army	Hargreaves, Grassington

DODGE WC53

The Dodge T214-WC53 introduced in 1942 was a ¾-ton 4×4 normal control vehicle with a wheelbase of 9 ft. 6 in. Given a Dodge T214 6-cylinder petrol engine of 92 bhp. it had a 4-speed gearbox and hydraulic brakes. The WC53 was fitted with either Command Field Sedan of Carryall bodywork and remained in production until 1945.

Examples Preserved.

	1943	Command Radio	US Army	Gray, Worthing
		Command Radio		Evans, Morecambe
		Command Radio		Rushton, Devon

DODGE WC54

The Dodge WC54 was always fitted with ambulance bodywork as shown here.

(K. A. Jenkinson)

Introduced in 1942, the WC54 is based on the ¾-ton Dodge T214 chassis, this being a normal control 4×4 with a wheelbase of 8 ft. 2 in. Powered by a 6-cylinder Dodge petrol engine of 92 bhp, it has a 4-speed gearbox and hydraulic brakes which act on all four wheels. Fitted with an all-steel, 4-stretcher ambulance body by Wayne, a number of later WC54's were used as vans or converted to open-cab. The WC54 was used by the British Army (Lend-Lease) and it remained in production until 1945.

Examples Preserved.

	1942	Ambulance	US Army	John, Bristol
305DEL	1942	Ambulance		Alexander, Bournemouth
GKE207T	1942	Ambulance		Blake, Southall
HYO320	1942	Ambulance	US Army	Beddall, Iver
J44875	1942	Ambulance	US Army	Stafford-Nelson, Jersey
RC9968	1942	Ambulance	US Army	Melia, Bolton

JCW396S	1943	Ambulance	US Army	Payne, Lancaster
MMY30	1943	Ambulance	US Army	Beddall, Iver
NGX999P	1943	Ambulance	US Army	Lovegrove, Bromley
YBP999L	1943	Ambulance	US Army	Warnham War Museum
FOU190K	1944	Ambulance	French Army	Gray, Worthing
	1943	Ambulance	US Army	Groom, Warlingham
	1943	Ambulance	US Army	Mills, Winchester
	1943	Ambulance	US Army	Mann, Lamanva
	1943	Ambulance		Jenkins, Kent
NMV499P	1944	Ambulance	US Army	Coult, Harrow
		Ambulance		Kirk, Lincoln
		Ambulance		Holmes, Kent
		Ambulance		Roberts, Salop

DODGE WC56

A Dodge WC56 command reconnaissance is seen here undergoing restoration.

(D. Game)

Built in the US, and first introduced in 1942, the WC56 is a 4 × 4 ¾-ton vehicle based on the Dodge T214 chassis. Of normal control layout, it has a wheelbase of 8 ft. 2 in. and is fitted with a Dodge 6-cylinder petrol engine of 92 bhp. with a bore and stroke of 3¼ in. × 4⅝ in. It has a 4-speed gearbox with a single speed transfer box whilst its brakes are of the hydraulic type, acting on all wheels. Command Reconnaissance type bodywork is fitted to the WC56 and it remained in production until 1945. The WC56 was one of the models used by the British Army (Lend-Lease) during World War II.

Examples Preserved.

PDM879	1942	Command Car	US Army	Hickman, Bobbington
JPP320	1942	Command Car	US Army	Oakford, Ickford

GPK67K	1943	Command Car	US Army	Groom, Warlingham
SNX824M	1943	Command Car	US Army	Fortnum, Rugby
YCK585R	1943	Command Car	US Army	Evans, Morcambe
YWJ210M	1943	Command Car	US Army	Moulson, Bradford
ERX507	1944	Command Car	US Army	Gray, Worthing
OBP523J	1944	Command Car	US Army	West, Worthing
		Command Car		Jones, Salop
		Command Car		West, Surrey
		Command Car	US Army	Dent, Hertford,
		Command Car		Houlahan & Busby Hook Norton
81543707		Command Car		Imperial War Museum, Duxford
		Command Car	US Army	Jones, Gwent
		Command Car	US Army	Priestley, Devon
	1944	Command Car	US Army	Mann, Lamanva
		Command Car		Kenten, London
		Command Car		Guy, Hants.
		Command Car		Foley, London
		Command Car		Chapman, Kettering
	1945	Command Car	US Army	Mann, Lamanva

DODGE WC57

The winch can be clearly seen on this Dodge WC57 command reconnaissance, CUD39.

(K. A. Jenkinson)

Basically similar to the WC56, the US built Dodge WC57 is a 4×4 ¾-tonner constructed on a T214 type chassis. Having a wheelbase of 8 ft. 2 in. it is of normal control design and uses a Dodge 6-cylinder petrol engine of 92 bhp. with 3¼ in. bore and 4⅝ in. stroke. Fitted with a 4-speed gearbox and single speed transfer box, it has hydraulically operated brakes which act on all four wheels. The WC57 has Command Reconnaissance bodywork with winch, and it continued to be produced until 1945. It was also used by the British Army (Lend-Lease) during the war.

Examples Preserved.

JGN348	1941	Command Car	US Army	Passey, Newbury
CUD39	1943	Command Car	US Army	Warnham War Museum
FUY270	1943	Command Car	US Army	Houlahan & Busby, Over Norton
		Command Car		Groom, Warlingham
	1944	Command Car		Cleaver, Chadlington

DODGE WC63

CDG623K, a 6×6 Dodge WC63 personnel truck restored in US Army livery.

(C. Pearce)

Based on the Dodge 1½-ton 6×6 T223 chassis, the US built WC63 is of normal control layout. Having a 10 ft. 5 in. wheelbase with 42 in. bogie centres it is powered by a Dodge 6-cylinder 92 bhp. petrol engine whilst transmission is via a 4-speed gearbox with 2-speed transfer box. The brakes are hydraulically operated and the WC63 which was introduced in 1942 carried truck bodywork for personnel and cargo purposes. It is also fitted with a winch and it remained in production until 1945.

Examples Preserved.

GBY109	1942	Personnel Carrier		Fowler, Basingstoke
LPH22D	1942	Weapons Carrier	USAF	Bashall, Guildford
LTW825	1944	Cargo Truck	USAF	Groom, Warlingham
	1944	Cargo Truck	US Army	Hamilton, Stirling
CDG623K	1944	Personnel Carrier	US Army	Private Owner

FERRET SCOUT CAR

Built by Daimler, the Ferret was a 4 × 4 scout car. OODD39 pictured here is a Mk.4 model of 1965 vintage.

(D. Game)

Developed by the Daimler company to meet a British Army requirement for a fast, light 4 × 4 scout car which could ford water to a depth of 3 ft. without protection, the Ferret went into production in 1951, entering service in the following year. Powered by a Rolls Royce B60, 129 bhp. 6-cylinder petrol engine, it is 11 ft. 1 in. long, 6 ft. 3 in. wide and 6 ft. 2 in. high. Since its introduction, it has been supplied to armies throughout the world. In 1964, the Ferret Mk.4 was introduced, this being basically similar to the earlier marks but being armed with a turret mounted .3 in. MG with an elevation of + 45° and a depression of − 15°. The Mk.5, being the last variant of the Ferret to be introduced, first appeared in 1966. This model, used only by the British army has larger wheels, modified suspension and a new turret of all welded aluminium construction. This has four launcher boxes, two on each side, for the Swingfire long-range anti-tank missile, a further two missiles being carried in reserve. In addition, 1 × 7.62 mm. MG is mounted in the front of the turret. The Ferret range was finally discontinued in 1971 by which time 4,409 had been built.

Examples Preserved.

Mk.4 00DD39	1965	Scout Car	Brit. Army	Imperial War Museum, Duxford
Mk.4 01DD08	1965	Scout Car	Brit. Army	RAC Museum, Bovington
Mk.5 03EE06	1967	Scout Car	Brit. Army	RAC Museum, Bovington
Mk.5 04BB65	1968	Scout Car	Brit. Army	Leyland Historic Vehicles Donington

FODEN DG6/12

Based upon a civillian model was the Foden DG6/12, a military example of which is shown here.
(Fodens Ltd.)

Introduced in 1941, the Foden 6/12 was a 10-ton 6 × 4 model of forward control layout. Having a wheelbase of 15 ft. 8 in., it was fitted with a Gardner 6LW 6-cylinder oil engine and had a 5-speed gearbox and triple-servo hydraulic brakes. Various types of body were fitted including Printing, GS, flat platform, and photographic. It remained in production until 1945.

Example Preserved.

| 1944 | Van | Brit. Army | RCT Museum, Driffield |

FODEN FE6/22

Shown here in British Army service is a Foden FE6 fitted with a standard Foden cab of the period.
(Fodens Ltd.)

The Foden FE6/22 was a 6×4 model of forward control layout built to carry a 10-ton payload. Powered by a Foden FD6 Mk.6 2-stroke 6-cylinder diesel engine, transmission was via a Foden 12-speed gearbox whilst the brakes were air operated. Also built for civilian use as a 16-ton lorry, the military vehicle was fitted with 'super single' rear wheels. Introduced in 1960, this model remained in production for ten years, being discontinued in 1970.

Example Preserved.

1962 G/S Lorry   Brit. Army   Rhodes, Arrington

FORD AFV MkVI

The sole survivor of the 28 Ford AFV Mk.VI's built, ZD1760 is depicted here awaiting restoration.
(P. Isaac)

Introduced in 1942, the Irish Ford AFV Mk.VI was designed by Col. J. V. Lawless and Comdt. A. W. Mayne in the Cavalry Workshops, Curragh Camp and were built by Thompson & Son Ltd., Hanover Works, Carlow. Powered by a Ford V8 petrol engine, the AFV Mk.VI was mounted with 1 × Vickers .303 machine gun. Only 28 were built, 11 of which were air-lifted to the Congo for U.N. duties.

Example Preserved.

ZD1760	1942	AFV	Isaac, Umberleigh

FORD F15

The Ford F15 was of Canadian Military Pattern, being 4 × 2 semi-forward control 15-cwt vehicle, introduced in 1940. Given an 8 ft. 5¼ in. wheelbase, it was powered by a Ford V8 petrol engine and 4-speed gearbox whilst its brakes were hydraulically operated acting on all four wheels. Numerous types of bodywork could be fitted and it remained in production until 1945.

Examples Preserved.

ELP200J	1942	Mobile Ack Ack	Brit. Army	Green, Warlingham
	1943		Brit. Army	Whitehead, Birmingham
	1943		Brit. Army	Jenkins, Kent
EKY291	1943	G/S Truck	Brit. Army	Moulson, Bradford
	1944		Brit. Army	Marchant, Milton Keynes

FORD F30

Built to Canadian standard pattern with No.13 cab is this Ford F30, seen here complete with canvas tilt.

(C. Pearce)

The Canadian built Ford F30 was introduced in 1940. Being a 30-cwt 4×4 model with semi-forward control layout, it had a wheelbase of 11 ft. 2¼ in. and was powered by a Ford V8 95 bhp. petrol engine. Transmission was via a 4-speed gearbox with 2-speed transfer box and the brakes were of the hydraulic type. GS, ambulance, derrick, winch truck or LAA tractor bodywork was fitted and the F30 remained in production until 1943.

Examples Preserved.

ACF255	1940	G/S Truck		Jackson, Wormingford
	1942	G/S Truck	Brit. Army	Speechy, Bucks.
JU054	1942	G/S Truck		Private Owner
	1942	G/S Truck	Brit. Army	Baxter, Surrey
413DEL	1942	G/S Truck	Brit. Army	Rowlands, Wetherby

FORD F60 4×4

JUO52 is a Canadian pattern Ford F60—a type which saw wide use during World War II.

(P. Isaac)

The Canadian Military Pattern Ford F60 was a semi-forward control 3-ton 4×4 model introduced in 1940. Three different wheelbase variants were built, the F60T having a measurement of 9 ft. 7¼ in., the F60S being 11 ft. 2¼ in. and the F60L 13 ft. 2¼ in. All were powered by a Ford V8 30 hp. petrol engine and had a 4-speed gearbox with 2-speed transfer box and hydraulic (hydrovac) brakes. Numerous different types of bodywork could be fitted to the F60S and F60L (the F60T being a tractor) and the models continued in production until 1945. A 4×2 version of the F60 was also built.

Examples Preserved.

F60S	1943	AA Tractor	Brit. Army	Fisher, Bucks.
F60S	1943	AA Tractor	Brit. Army	Pearce, Holywell
F60S	1944	AA Tractor	Brit. Army	Charman, Market Rasen
F60S	1944	G/S Truck	Brit. Army	Mankin, Heddon on the Wall
F60S JU052	1944	AA Tractor	Brit. Army	Isaac, Umberleigh
F60S	1944			Warnham War Museum
F60S	1944	AA Tractor	Brit. Army	Meikle, Durham
F60S	1944	AA Tractor	Brit. Army	Wilson, Hexham
F60S	1944	AA Tractor	Brit. Army	Mann, Lamanva

FORD GP

A very rare marque of jeep is the Ford GP of which only 3,650 were built. MYH245 depicted here has been authentically restored in US Army colours.

(K. A. Jenkinson)

Making its debut in 1941, the Ford GP was US built, being a ¼-ton normal control 4 × 4 model. With 6 ft. 8 in. wheelbase and Ford 4-cylinder 45 bhp. petrol engine, it has a 3-speed gearbox with 2-speed transfer box and hydraulic brakes. The engine used was a specially adapted Ford tractor engine. Command reconnaissance bodywork was fitted, and around 3,650 were built before the GP was discontinued at the end of 1941.

Examples Preserved.

	1941	Jeep	Brit. Army	Brindley, Wolverhampton
5634AH	1941	Jeep		Beddall, Iver
MYH245	1941	Jeep	Brit. Army	Lake, Stockton

FORD GPA

The Ford GPA was an amphibious jeep. HLA383 illustrated here was built in 1942.

(C. Pearce)

The Ford GPA was the amphibious version of the Jeep GPW and it entered production in September 1942. It had a wheelbase of 7 ft. 0 in. and was given a Ford GPW442 4-cylinder engine of 54 bhp., a 3-speed gearbox with 2-speed transfer box and hydraulic brakes. A ¼-ton 4×4 model, it had only a short production life, being discontinued later in 1942.

Examples Preserved.

FFY610D	1942	Amphibious Jeep	US Army	Pressdee, Mumbles
HLA383	1942	Amphibious Jeep	US Army	Gray, Worthing
	1942	Amphibious Jeep	US Army	Warnham War Museum
	1942	Amphibious Jeep	US Army	Marchant, Milton Keynes
	1942	Amphibious Jeep	US Army	Shaw, Southall
	1942	Amphibious Jeep	US Army	Jenkins, Cardiff

FORD GPW

The popular 'jeep' was built by Ford and Willys. FAF622L is a Ford example dating from 1945.
(C. Pearce)

Built in the US, the Ford GPW was first introduced in 1942. A 4 × 4 ¼ ton model of normal control layout, the GPW is perhaps better known as the Jeep. Given a 6 ft. 8 in. wheelbase, it is powered by a 54 bhp. 4-cylinder petrol engine and has a 3-speed gearbox with 2-speed transfer box and hydraulic brakes which act on all four wheels. Produced to Willys MB design but having inverted U-section front chassis cross member (the Willys MB used a tubular section), 277,896 were built before production ended in 1945. The GPW was used by all the United Nations and whilst all were fitted with reconnaissance car bodywork, a small number were later modified for use as ambulances.

Examples Preserved.

676WU	1942	Jeep		Hirst, Wakefield
SWM221	1942	Jeep		Holt, Carlisle
AK30	1942	Jeep		Kennedy, Rochdale
CYV7H	1942	Jeep	US Army	Falce, London
FOT307	1942	Jeep		Fry, Barry
GDG599	1942	Jeep		West, Worthing
GLJ706	1942	Jeep		Private Owner
LPF904	1942	Jeep		MT Pres. Group, Croydon
	1942	Jeep		Matthews, Huddersfield
THO128	1942	Jeep	US Army	Mann, Lamanva
UXN792	1942	Jeep	US Army	Tallents, Kidderminster
YMC978	1942	Jeep		Lamb, Thatcham
5634AH	1942	Jeep		Beddall, Iver
982GOG	1942	Jeep	US Army	Egerton, Morton in Marsh
107SPL	1942	Jeep		Guy, Ringwood

	1942	Jeep		Williamson, Winchester
	1942	Jeep		Wright, Worksop
	1942	Jeep		Hart, Wadhurst
	1942	Jeep		Gowers, Chelmsford
	1942	Jeep		Dudley, Birmingham
	1942	Jeep		Saunders, Farmoor
	1942	Jeep		Needham, Nottingham
	1942	Jeep		Winter, Bristol
	1942	Jeep		Boulton, Taunton
CPC962	1942	Jeep		Evans, Brighton
PYY130	1942	Jeep		Private Owner
	1943	Jeep	US Army	Golding, Bristol
RBU126	1943	Jeep	US Army	Slater, Oldham
EHR234	1943	Jeep		Gray, Worthing
ENP381	1943	Jeep		Southey, Warminster
FAF622L	1943	Jeep	US Army	Mann, Lamanva
GCV722	1943	Jeep		Johnson, Wythall
HXW136	1943	Jeep	Brit. Army	Parish, Oswestry
JYD287	1943	Jeep		Staddon, Marlborough
KAA751	1943	Jeep	Brit. Army	Elliott-Smith, Bexley
KPM74	1943	Jeep	US Army	Kent, Hertford
PHN430	1943	Jeep	US Army	Arthurs, Durham
RLF25	1943	Jeep		Hall, Durham
WLL869	1943	Jeep	US Army	Vanderveen, Holland
XLA711	1943	Jeep		Black, Keighley
YDU836	1943	Jeep		Warnham War Museum
1376FS	1943	Jeep		Cremer, Edinburgh
15YH75	1943	Jeep	Brit. Army	Brindley, Wolverhampton
390DDV	1943	Jeep	US Army	Petchey, Winchcombe
	1943	Jeep		Thomas, Attleborough
MAD618	1943	Jeep		James, Evesham
	1943	Jeep		Pearce, Holywell
	1943	Jeep		Jones, Caerwent
	1943	Jeep		Groves, Didcot
304971	1943	Jeep		Hofman, Highworth
	1943	Jeep		Bossons, London
8264VP	1943	Jeep		Marchant, Milton Keynes
SMG46	1943	Jeep		Himmins, Hove
	1943	Jeep		Walmsley, Gallywood
	1943	Jeep		Barker, London
	1943	Jeep		Robinson, Burton Latimer
	1943	Jeep		Dowdall, London
	1943	Jeep		Green, London
	1943	Jeep		Kirk, Lincoln
HAK888E	1943	Jeep		Moulson, Bradford
	1943	Jeep		Young, Leeds
	1943	Jeep		Le Conte, Jersey
	1943	Jeep		Gorfield, Liverpool
	1943	Jeep		Clifford, London
	1943	Jeep		Ellis, Reading
	1943	Jeep		Slomczynski, Hanwood
	1943	Jeep		Pearson, Leicester
FOU965	1944	Jeep		Davies, Cardiff
GAP951	1944	Jeep		Arnold, Kent
HBP997H	1944	Jeep		Mann, Lamanva
HBP998H	1944	Jeep		Warnham War Museum
JB9481	1944	Jeep		Miles, Barnstable

JKP809	1944	Jeep		Private Owner
MAD618	1944	Jeep		Pascoe, Southsea
NPM934	1944	Jeep		MacDonald, Inverness
	1944	Jeep		Coult, Harrow
	1944	Jeep		Davies, Frome
	1944	Jeep		McIntyre, Sorn Castle
OHW87	1944	Jeep		Staddon, Marlborough
UOT519	1944	Jeep		Short, Dorset
WOT538	1944	Jeep	Brit. Army	Corfield, Liverpool
XCY7	1944	Jeep		Pressdee, Mumbles
	1944	Jeep		Batey, Stanley
	1944	Jeep		Bishop, Birmingham
	1944	Jeep		Curwen, Newcastle upon Tyne
	1944	Jeep		Vincent, Reading
	1944	Jeep		Bowman, Blaydon
	1944	Jeep		Lewis, Abergavenny
TN0946	1944	Jeep		Hamilton, Old Plean
	1944	Jeep		Taverner, Cardiff
TNT610	1944	Jeep	US Army	Hodge, Blyth
	1944	Jeep		Linsley, Stokesley
	1944	Jeep		Chedzoy, Newcastle upon Tyne
	1944	Jeep		Thompson, Alnwick
	1944	Jeep		Houlahan, Hook Norton
	1944	Jeep		Groombridge, Heathfield
	1944	Jeep		Wight, Pullham St. Mary
	1944	Jeep		Kenten, London
	1944	Jeep		Skinner, Twickenham
	1944	Jeep		Pierce Jones, Crowthorne
	1944	Jeep		Simmers, Aberdeen
EMY857	1945	Jeep		Private Owner
HYC15	1945	Jeep		Bolton, Somerset
KPP397	1945	Jeep		Dabbs, Ripley
	1945	Jeep		Lake, Stockton
UGV102J	1945	Jeep		James, Ixworth
349FKJ	1945	Jeep		Private Owner
938LTD	1945	Jeep		Private Owner
	1945	Jeep		Alexander, London
	1945	Jeep		Beckwith, Kirkby Stephen
	1945	Jeep		Walmsley, Galleywood
	1945	Jeep		Payne, Hest Bank
	1945	Jeep		Wardale, Washington
WLL869	1945	Jeep		Private Owner
	1945	Jeep		Ramsey, Rowlands Gill
FWK529	1945	Jeep		Mill, Kempson
	1945	Jeep		Beaton, Inverness
JOD820	1945	Jeep		Avon Commercial Recovery, Severn Beach

FORD GTB

Produced chiefly for the US Navy, the Ford GTB was the only low silhouette type truck to enter series production. Introduced in 1942 it was a 30-cwt 4×4 model of normal control layout with a wheelbase of 9 ft. 7 in. Powered by a Ford 6-cylinder 90 bhp. petrol engine it had a 4-speed gearbox with 2-speed transfer box. 6,000 of this model were built fitted with cargo or bomb service bodywork and the GTB was discontinued at the end of 1942.

Example Preserved.

NTW444	G/S Cargo	US Navy	Webb, Bishops Stortford

FORD T16 UNIVERSAL CARRIER

Built throughout the whole of World War II, the Universal Carrier has survived into preservation. One of the examples to be seen at rallies is T296765 shown here.

(C. Pearce)

Introduced in 1939, the Universal Bren Carrier was produced in vast quantities in several countries including USA, where it was designated the T16. Its hull was a simple steel box with the engine set in the middle, it being driven by tracks with three road wheels on each side, suspended by coil springs. Its driving controls were identical to those of a lorry and it was powered by a Ford V8 petrol engine, with a 4-speed gearbox. Being 12 ft. 4 in. long, 6 ft. 11 in. wide and 5 ft. 3 in. high, it was armed with 1 × Bren LMG or 1 × Boys anti-tank rifle. Around 35,000 were built in the United Kingdom, 5,600 in Australia, 520 in New Zealand, over 29,000 in Canada and 13,893 in USA before production ended in 1945.

Examples Preserved.

T296765	1942	Bren Carrier	Brit. Army	Groombridge, Heathfield
T273546	1943	Bren Carrier	Brit. Army	Warnham War Museum

	1943	Bren Carrier	Brit. Army	Miller, Lincoln
	1943	Bren Carrier	Brit. Army	Blyth, Holt
	1943	Bren Carrier	Brit. Army	Mann, Lamanva
	1944	Bren Carrier	Brit. Army	Pearce, Holywell
	1944	Bren Carrier	Brit. Army	Mansell, Pershore
	1944	Bren Carrier	Brit. Army	Anderson, Otterburn
	1944	Bren Carrier	Brit. Army	Busby & Houlahan, Hook Norton
	1945	Bren Carrier	Brit. Army	Pearce, Holywell
	1945	Bren Carrier	Brit. Army	Venners, Wantage
		Bren Carrier	Brit. Army	Caley, Saxmundham
		Bren Carrier	Brit. Army	Imperial War Museum, London
		Bren Carrier	Brit. Army	Mankin, Heddon on the Wall
74ZT15		Bren Carrier	Brit. Army	DLI Museum, Durham

FORD THAMES E-Series

The Ford Thames E Series was fitted with a Commer-type cab as can be seen on this Duple bodied office vehicle.

(Duple Coachbuilders Ltd.)

The Ford Thames E-Series was introduced in 1951 and was of the 3-ton 4×4 type of forward control layout. Given a wheelbase of 12 ft. 6 in., the power unit used was a Ford V8 8-cylinder petrol engine of 87 bhp. whilst transmission was via a 4-speed gearbox with 2-speed transfer box. A Commer-type cab was fitted and bodywork could be of the light anti-aircraft tractor, ambulance, office or stores type, the coachbuilders used including Mulliner, Spurling and Duple.

Example Preserved.

1954	Office Van	Brit. Army	Dudley, London

FORD WOA2

Authentically restored to its military specification, the Ford WOA2 was widely used by the British Army during World War II.

(C. Pearce)

The British built Ford WOA2 was first introduced in May 1941. Being a 4×2 heavy utility of normal control layout, it has a wheelbase of 9 ft. 0¼ in. Powered by a Ford V8 petrol engine of 3.6 litres capacity with a bore and stroke of 3.96 in. × 3.75 in., it has a 3-speed gearbox and single dry plate clutch to a ¾ floating, spiral bevel rear axle. Its brakes are mechanically operated acting on all wheels. It has 6-seater bodywork with four side doors and full width split rear doors, although some were modified and fitted with canvas tilt. The WOA2 continued in production until July 1944.

Examples Preserved.

M3759081	1941	Heavy Utility	Brit. Army	Private Owner
	1941	Heavy Utility	Brit. Army	Warnham War Museum
OBW745	1943	Heavy Utility	Brit. Army	Venners, Reading
GXT672	1944	Heavy Utility	Brit. Army	Groombridge, Heathfield
	1944	Heavy Utility	Brit. Army	Mann, Lamanva

FORDSON WOT1

Introduced in 1940, the Ford WOT1 was a 3-ton 6×4 normal control vehicle originally built with a 13 ft. 8½ in. wheelbase, this later being altered to 13 ft. 10½ in. Powered by a Ford V8 petrol engine of 85 bhp., it had a 4-speed gearbox and mechanically operated brakes. Standardised upon by the RAF for use as ambulances, the WOT1 was also fitted with crew coach and recruiting office bodywork and remained in production until 1943.

Examples Preserved.

1941	Fire Engine	RAF	Corbin, Duxford
1942		RAF	Mann, Lamanva
1942	Van	RAF	Vince, Ely

FORD WOT2

The Ford WOT2 was a 4×2 15cwt model an example of which is shown here in the form of ONH681P.

(C. Pearce)

Built at Dagenham, the Ford WOT2 was a 15 cwt. 4×2 model with normal control layout. It had a wheelbase of 8 ft. 10 in. and was fitted with a Ford V8 petrol engine rated at 30 hp. with a bore and stroke of 77.79 mm. × 95.25 mm. Transmission was via a 4-speed gearbox and single dry plate clutch to a fully floating spiral bevel rear axle. Mechanically operated brakes acted on all 4 wheels. Introduced in 1940, several types of bodywork could be fitted and the WOT2 remained in production until 1944.

Examples Preserved.

FLA248C	1943	G/S Truck	Brit. Army	Oliver, Eton Wick
FMC428C	1943	G/S Truck	Brit. Army	Oliver, Eton Wick

	1943		Brit. Army	Venners, Oxon
	1943		Brit. Army	Marchant, Milton Keynes
	1943		Brit. Army	James, Worcester
	1943		Brit. Army	Sayer, Suffolk
	1943	G/S Truck	Brit. Army	Edgerton, Warwicks
	1943		Brit. Army	Bashall, Surrey
	1943		Brit. Army	Payne, Hest Bank
	1943	G/S Truck	Brit. Army	Robinson, Burton Latimer
KOE514P	1944	G/S Truck	Brit. Army	Wadsworth, Godalming
	1944	G/S Truck	Brit. Army	Robinson, Burton Latimer
ONH681P	1944	G/S Truck	Brit. Army	Private Owner

FORD WOT3

First produced towards the end of 1940, the Ford WOT3 was a normal control 4 × 2 30 cwt model supplied to both the Army and the RAF with a variety of bodywork. Having a wheelbase of 11 ft. 11½ in. it was powered by a Ford V8 30 hp. petrol engine and had a 4-speed gearbox and mechanically operated brakes. The WOT3 remained in production until 1944 and some were supplied to the Indian Army with open cabs.

Examples Preserved.

1943	Tractor		Warnham War Museum
1943	G/S Truck	Brit. Army	Mankin, Heddon on the Wall

FORDSON WOT6

32YX84, seen here as if waiting for its next engagement, is a Ford WOT6.

(D. Game)

Making its debut in January 1942, the Fordson WOT6 was a 3-ton 4×4 vehicle of forward control layout. Given a wheelbase of 11 ft. 11½ in. it was powered by a Ford V8 85 bhp. petrol engine and had a 4-speed gearbox with 2-speed transfer box. More usually fitted with GS bodywork it was also built with various types of machinery bodies. It continued in production until September 1945.

Examples Preserved.

	1942	G/S Truck	Brit. Army	Mann, Lamanva
RMG773R	1943	Machinery	Brit. Army	Webb, Bishops Stortford
	1943	Machinery	Brit. Army	Harper, Attleborough
32YX84	1944	G/S Truck	Brit. Army	Imperial War Museum, Duxford

FORDSON 7V

This Fordson 7V tractor was used by Field Marshal Montgomery to draw one of his trailer caravans during World War II.

(K. A. Jenkinson)

Introduced as a civilian model in 1937, the Fordson 7V was a 4×2, 4-6 ton model with forward control layout. Given a choice of 9 ft. 10 in., 10 ft. 2 in., 10 ft. 8 in. or 13 ft. 1 in. wheelbase it was available with either a Ford 4-cylinder 3285 cc. petrol engine or a Ford V8 petrol engine of 3622 cc. The vast majority of 7V's used by the armed forces used the V8 engine. Transmission was via a 4-speed gearbox whilst the brakes were mechanically operated. The 7V's supplied for military use were mainly used as tipping trucks although they were also used in a number of other roles including tractor units for coupling to semi-trailers. The 7V remained in production until 1949.

Examples Preserved.

1944	Tractor & Caravan Brit. Army	Imperial War Museum, London
1944	Chassis/cab	Imperial War Museum, Duxford

FOX

The Fox is a combat reconnaissance 4 × 4 vehicle, the prototype of which first appeared in November 1967. Although this was built by Daimler, all the production vehicles were built at the ROF at Leeds, the first ones being completed in May 1973. Powered by a Jaguar 4.2 litre 6-cylinder petrol engine, the Fox is armed with 1 × 30 mm. Rarden cannon and 1 × 7.62 mm. co-axial MG 2 × 4 barrelled smoke dischargers are fitted, as is a full range of day and night driving vision and fire control devices. A floatation screen is carried round the top of the hull which can be quickly erected and the Fox still remains in production.

Example Preserved.

OOSP89   1970   Reconnaissance   Brit. Army   RAC Museum, Bovington

FV432

One of the prototype FV432's has now been preserved and is seen here at the Warnham War Museum.

(K. A. Jenkinson)

Introduced in 1963, the FV432 Armoured Personnel Carrier was built by GKN Sankey at Wellington, Shropshire. Designed to carry a crew of 2 plus 10 other personnel, it is powered by a Rolls Royce K60 6-cylinder multi-fuel engine. Of 17 ft. 3 in. length, 9 ft. 2 in. width and 7 ft. 6 in. height, it is armed with 1 × 7.62 mm. general purpose MG. Having six road wheels on each side, the FV432 has been adapted for numerous roles, each of which was given its own designation number. It remained in production until 1971 and a number are still in use with the British army where it is expected they will serve until the 1980's.

Example Preserved.

157BXR   1963   APC   Brit. Army   Warnham War Museum

FWD HAR 1

Introduced in 1942, the FWD HAR 1 was a normal control 4-ton 4 × 4 model. Given a 13 ft. 0 in. wheelbase, it was powered by a Waukesha 6-cylinder petrol engine of 88 bhp. Transmission was via a 5-speed gearbox with 2-speed transfer box whilst the brakes were of the hydraulic hydrovac type. For the US Forces, the HAR 1 was fitted with cargo bodywork whereas the RAF used it for smoke generating and snow-fighting purposes. For the latter, a Bros rotary snowplough was fitted to the front of the chassis, this being driven by a Climax R6 engine mounted on the chassis frame behind the cab. The FWD HAR 1 was unusual in having permanent four-wheel drive and it remained in production until 1944.

Example Preserved.

1943	G/S Truck	US Army	Logue, Duddenhoe End

GMC CCKW-352

Dating from 1943, SAP23N is a GMC CCKW-352 Cargo truck once used by the U.S.Army.
(K. A. Jenkinson)

The American built GMC CCKW-352 was a 2½ ton 6 × 6 vehicle first introduced in 1941. Given a wheelbase of 12 ft. 1 in., it was powered by a GMC 6-cylinder petrol engine and had a 5-speed gearbox with 2-speed transfer box. Of normal control layout, it was available with various types of bodywork including cargo, bomb service, dump or tanker. The CCKW-352 remained in production until 1945.

Examples Preserved.

VBP179N	1942	Cargo Truck	US Army	Deadman, Farnham
CFK815	1943	Personnel Carrier	US Army	Theobald, Warnham
SAP23N	1943	Cargo Truck	US Army	Lyndhurst, Warnham
VFL216	1943	Cargo Truck	French Army	Marshall, Huntingdon
	1943	Cargo Truck		Chapman, Kettering
	1943	Cargo Truck		Mann, Lamanva

GMC CCKWX-353

CWJ612T, a GMC CCKW-353 G/S truck shows the early style of open cab fitted to American trucks built during the early part of World War II.

(K. A. Jenkinson)

The GMC CCKWX-353 was a 2½ ton 6×6 normal control cargo truck introduced in 1941. Given a wheelbase of 13 ft. 8 in. it used a GMC 104 bhp. 6-cylinder petrol engine and had a 5-speed gearbox with 2-speed transfer box. Its brakes were of the hydrovac type and the CCKWX-353 was discontinued in 1945.

Examples Preserved.

CWJ612T	1941	Cargo Truck	US Army	Mallinson, Rotherham
	1941	Cargo Truck	US Army	Taylor, Poole
27YBP	1941	Recovery	US Army	Lyons, Guildford
CFA879	1941	Cargo Truck	US Army	Bishop, Yardley
	1941	Tipper		Goodman, Southam
	1941	Cargo Truck		Chapman, Kettering
GMS238S	1941	Cargo Truck	French Army	Hamilton, Stirling
	1941	Tipper	US Army	Phelps, Longhope
	1942	Cargo Truck		Wilkinson, Ringwood
	1942	Dump Truck		Chapman, Kettering
MLA963	1943		US Army	Gray, Worthing
	1943	Cargo Truck	US Army	Baker, Stowmarket
	1943	Cargo Truck		Mann, Lamanva
	1943	Cargo Truck	US Army	Reed, Shepton Mallet
	1943	Cargo Truck		Davidson, Otford
	1943	Cargo Truck	US Army	James, Evesham
27YPB	1943	Cargo Truck		Lyons, Guildford
ECJ216	1943	Cargo Truck		Warnham War Museum
	1943		US Army	Goddard, Southam
	1943		US Army	Bret, Andrews Field
	1943	Tanker		Mann, Lamanva
	1943	Cargo Truck	US Army	Millman, Devon
	1943	Cargo Truck		Standeven, Avon
	1943	Tanker		Chapman, Kettering
	1944	Cargo Truck		Mann, Lamanva

	1944	Cargo Truck		Jenkins, Kent
JKJ35L	1944	Cargo Truck		Private Owner
	1944	Cargo Truck	US Army	Pettle, Mansfield

GMC DUKW

Used as a landing craft during World War II, the GMC DUKW is an amphibious vehicle with a boat-like hull as shown here.

(K. A. Jenkinson)

Nicknamed 'Duck', the GMC DUKW-353 was a 6×6, 2½-ton amphibious vehicle, first introduced in 1942. Fitted with a GMC 6-cylinder petrol engine of 104 bhp. it had an engine-driven propeller and 5-speed gearbox with 2-speed transfer box. It had a 13 ft. 8 in. wheelbase and was supplied to US and Allied Armies. Production ended in 1945.

Examples Preserved.

	1942	Amphibian	US Army	Warnham War Museum
MYY486P	1942	Amphibian		Beddall, Iver
SUJ917S	1942	Amphibian	US Army	Froggatt, Ludlow
NYH279E	1942	Amphibian		Hamilton-Fish, Windlesham
	1942	Amphibian		Bowman, Newcastle
804DXV	1943	Amphibian	US Army	Griffiths, Warrington
DPX699L	1943	Amphibian	US Army	Gray, Worthing
	1943	Amphibian	US Army	Pearce, Holywell
PJB79R	1943	Amphibian	US Army	Ward, Pangbourne
XJA603S	1943	Amphibian		Marshall, Upton
	1943	Amphibian		Swift, Hants.
	1943	Amphibian		Jones, Salop
	1943	Amphibian		Oakford, Princes Risborough
74YP00	1943	Amphibian	Brit. Army	Imperial War Museum, Duxford
	1944	Amphibian	Brit. Army	RCT, Southampton
	1944	Amphibian		Mann, Lamanva
76YP19	1944	Amphibian	Brit. Army	Imperial War Museum, Duxford
	1945	Amphibian	Brit. Army	RCT, Aldershot
	1945	Amphibian	US Army	Tombs, Hants.
	1945	Amphibian		Seabury, Salop
	1945	Amphibian		Wilson, Hexham
	1945	Amphibian		McIntyre, Sorn Castle

GOLIATH

Named the Goliath, this tiny tracked vehicle was remotely controlled as a demolition vehicle.

(K. A. Jenkinson)

Originally intended for attacking tanks and pill boxes etc., the Goliath was the first and smallest of the German demolition vehicles. Introduced in February 1944, it was built by Bergward. Its body was divided into three units—the front containing explosives, the centre having 4 relays for controlling the 2×24 v. electric motors used for detonating the charge whilst the rear section contained a drum of 3-core remote control cable. Although tracked, the Goliath could not travel over very rough terrain and was vulnerable from small arms fire. It was remotely controlled and the operator was provided with a control box which contained switches and batteries. The Goliath was built until 1945.

Examples Preserved.

1944	Demolition	Ger. Army	RAC Museum, Bovington
1944	Demolition	Ger. Army	Imperial War Museum, London
1944	Demolition	Ger. Army	Kenton, London

GRANT

T24689, a Grant tank which saw service with the British Army is seen here in its preserved condition.
(K. A. Jenkinson)

The M3 series Medium Tank consisted of a number of production variants and special purpose developments, the first of which was the M3 Grant. A pilot model was built in April 1941 with full-scale production having been started by August of that year. Built by Detroit Arsenal, American Loco, Baldwin, Pressed Steel and Pullman, a total of 4,924 were built before production ceased in August 1942. Designed to carry a crew of six, the M3 had a riveted hull, side doors and was used by the USA Army. The version supplied to the British Army was given the name Grant I (after General Ulysses S. Grant). These were given a new cast turret to meet British requirements and the first arrived in the early part of 1942. Armament was provided by 1×75 mm. gun, 1×37 mm. gun and $3\text{-}4 \times .30$ cal. Browning MG. Powered by a Continental R-975 340 hp. engine, the Grant I was 18 ft. 6 in. long, 8 ft. 11 in. wide and 9 ft. 4 in. high.

Example Preserved.

T24689	1942	Tank	Brit. Army	RAC Museum, Bovington

GREYHOUND

Built in the USA for the British Army, the Greyhound was a 6×6 built towards the end of World War II.

(K. A. Jenkinson)

At the end of 1943 the American light armoured car M8 came into service. When supplied to the British army, this took the name Greyhound. Being a 6×6 vehicle and powered by a Hercules 6-cylinder JXD-type engine, it was armed with 1×37 mm. gun and 1×.30 in. co-axial Browning MG. It weighed 7.6 tons and remained in production until 1944.

Example Preserved.

1943	Armoured Car	Brit. Army	RAC Museum, Bovington

GUY ANT

Introduced in 1936, the Guy Ant is a 4×2 normal control 15-cwt. model. It has an 8 ft. 5 in. wheelbase and is powered by a Meadows 4-cylinder petrol engine of 3.68 litres capacity with a bore and stroke of 95 mm. × 130 mm. Transmission is by means of a 4-speed gearbox and single dry plate clutch to a fully floating, spiral bevel rear axle. The brakes are mechanically operated with both the foot and hand brakes acting on all 4-wheels. General Service type bodywork was fitted, and the Guy Ant remained in production until 1945.

Examples Preserved.

	1936	G/S Truck	Brit. Army	Miles, Shaftesbury
HXX604	1937	G/S Truck	Brit. Army	Hayward, Coulsdon
HBH316		G/S Truck	Brit. Army	WETC, Winkleigh
		G/S Truck	Brit. Army	Groombridge, Heathfield
		G/S Truck	Brit. Army	Rossbotham, Clwyd
	1941	G/S Truck	Brit. Army	Grisdale, Rufford

GUY FBAX

Introduced in 1933, the Guy FBAX was a forward control 3-ton 6×4 vehicle with a wheelbase of 12 ft. 6 in. Fitted with a Meadows 4-cylinder 5.1 litre petrol engine, it had a 4-speed gearbox with 2-speed transfer box and mechanical servo assisted brakes. In addition to being available with GS bodywork, it was also built with special bodies such as bridging, breakdown recovery, mobile crane, printing press, searchlight and wireless. It remained in production until 1944.

Examples Preserved.

DPR779	1933	Recovery	Brit. Army	Miles, Shaftesbury

GUY Mk.I

The Guy Mk.I armoured car was first introduced in prototype form in 1938. With a length of 13 ft. 6 in., width of 6 ft. 9 in. and height of 7 ft. 6 in., its design was based on the Guy Quad-Ant field artillery tractor chassis and was a 4×4 vehicle. Powered by a Meadows petrol engine of 53 bhp., it carried a crew of 3 and was armed with 1 × Vickers 0.5 in. MG and 1 × Vickers 0.303 in. MG. The Guy Mk.I went into production in 1940 and a total of 50 had been built when the Mk.IA was introduced later in the same year.

Example Preserved.

	1938	Armoured Car	Brit. Army	RAC Museum, Bovington

GUY QUAD ANT

Introduced towards the end of 1937, the Guy Quad Ant was a 4×4 vehicle with a wheelbase of 8 ft. 5 in. Its power unit was a Meadows 4-cylinder petrol engine of 58 bhp. whilst transmission was via a 4-speed gearbox. Originally built as a field artillery tractor, the Quad Ant remained in production in this form until 1943 after which time it was built solely as a G/S truck, finally being discontinued in 1944.

Examples Preserved.

		Artillery Tractor	Brit. Army	Groombridge, Heathfield
JDG281	1941	Artillery Tractor	Brit. Army	Lovegrove & Walmsley, Chelmsford

HALLFORD

Designed in 1912, the Hallford 3-ton lorry was of normal control layout and had a wheelbase of 12 ft. 0 in. Powered by a Dorman 4-cylinder petrol engine rated at 30 hp., it had a 4-speed sliding-pinion gearbox, cone clutch and chain final drive. Its brakes consisted of a transmission brake and rear wheel brakes. Cast steel wheels with solid rubber tyres were standard and the Hallford remained in production until 1917.

Example Preserved.

1914	D/S Truck	Brit. Army	Banfield, Staplehurst

HARRY HOPKINS

T119223, this preserved Harry Hopkins tank was built in 1941.

(K. A. Jenkinson)

Originally known as 'Tank, Light Mk.VII, revised', the Mk.VIII was designed by Vickers in 1941 as an improved version of the Mk.VII. Three prototypes were built based on the Mk.VII but having a revised faceted hull and turret, increased armour and hydraulically assisted steering. Metropolitan Cammell undertook production and 99 were completed by 1944. Its general characteristics were the same as the Tetrarch, but the Harry Hopkins never entered service as the British light tank requirement was by 1944 limited only to the airborne division, for which stocks of the Tetrarch were adequate. The Harry Hopkins carried a crew of 3, was 14 ft. 0 in. long, 8 ft. 10½ in. wide and 6 ft. 11 in. high. Its armament consisted of 1 × 2 pdr. OQF and 1 × 7.92 mm. Besa MG. The engine used in the Harry Hopkins was a Meadows 12-cylinder 148 hp. unit.

Example Preserved.

T119223	1941	Tank	Brit. Army	RAC Museum, Bovington

HILLMAN 10 hp.

Looking resplendent following its complete restoration is MXK961, a Hillman utility dating from 1942.

(K. A. Jenkinson)

Making its debut at the end of 1939, the Hillman 4 × 2 light utility, based on the Hillman Minx car has a wheelbase of 7 ft. 8 in. Having normal control layout, it uses a Hillman 4-cylinder petrol engine of 10 hp. with a bore and stroke of 63 mm. × 95 mm., and has a 4-speed gearbox, single dry plate clutch and semi-floating spiral bevel rear axle. Its brakes are mechanically operated, acting on all four wheels. Closed van or utility bodywork was fitted, and the Hillman remained in production until 1944.

Examples Preserved.

RBX231	1939	Utility		Whitehouse, Cheltenham
HUC607	1941	Utility	M.O.S.	Hill, Crawley
814AKT	1941	Utility		Groombridge, Heathfield
MXK961	1942	Utility	Brit. Army	Oxford Military Vehicle Associates
SAJ632	1943	Utility		Mann, Lamanva
VDD95	1943	Utility	Brit. Army	Warnham War Museum
89RD61	1944	Utility	Brit. Army	Bayles, London
	1944	Utility	Brit. Army	Worthing, Salop
	1944	Utility		Elgey, Peterlee

HOTCHKISS M201

Built in France under licence from Willys, the Hotchkiss M201 was first introduced in 1953. A 4×4, ¼-ton jeep, it had a wheelbase of 2.03 m. and was powered by a 4-cylinder petrol engine of 30 bhp., having a 3-speed gearbox with 2-speed transfer box. In appearance it closely resembled Willys' World War II MB-type jeep and with various modifications, the M201 remained in production until 1969.

Example Preserved.

1969	Jeep		Scott, Upper Longdon

HUMBER FWD

Used mainly by the British Army, the Humber FWD was an 8-cwt 4×4 generally fitted with heavy utility (personnel) bodywork.

(Chrysler Ltd.)

The Humber 8 cwt. 4×4 was first built in 1941 and was of normal control layout. Having a wheelbase of 9 ft. 3¾ in. it was fitted with a Humber 6-cylinder 26.88 hp. petrol engine and had a 4-speed gearbox with 2-speed transfer box. Its brakes were hydraulically operated and acted on all 4 wheels. The Humber 4×4 could be fitted with personnel, GS, heavy utility, ambulance or staff car bodywork and it remained in production until 1944.

Examples Preserved.

843FUF	1942	Heavy Utility	Brit. Army	Wadsworth, Godalming
CPO645G	1942	Heavy Utility	Brit. Army	Belsey, Storrington

M2594165	1942	Heavy Utility	Brit. Army	Gardiner, Bognor Regis
NBP91	1942	Heavy Utility	Brit. Army	Mitchell, Midhurst
	1942	Heavy Utility	Brit. Army	Marchant, Milton Keynes
	1942	Heavy Utility	Brit. Army	Copeland, Dorset
XS9965	1942	Heavy Utility	Brit. Army	Seabrook, Saffron Walden
	1942	Heavy Utility	Brit. Army	Whitehouse, Cheltenham
	1942	Personnel Carrier	Brit. Army	Hofman, Wilts
JUR692	1943	Heavy Utility	Brit. Army	Lewis, Gt. Yeldham
425JMV	1943	Heavy Utility	Brit. Army	Busby, Hook Norton
	1943	Heavy Utility	Brit. Army	Honeychurch, Salop
	1943	Heavy Utility	Brit. Army	Holmes, Surrey
	1943	Heavy Utility	Brit. Army	Mann, Lamanva
	1943	Heavy Utility	Brit. Army	Oliver, Egham
8714F	1944	Heavy Utility	Brit. Army	Oxford Military Vehicle Associates
4248WD	1944	Heavy Utility	Brit. Army	Chapman, Stockton on Tees.

HUMBER FV1601

The Humber FV1601 was built as a cargo vehicle during the early 'fifties. Preserved example WBH611J is seen here.

(C. Pearce)

Introduced in 1952, the Humber FV1601 was a 4×4, 1-ton vehicle of normal control layout with a wheelbase of 9 ft. 0 in. Powered by a Rolls Royce 6-cylinder B60-type 4250 cc. petrol engine it had a 5-speed gearbox and single speed transfer box with power take off. Its brakes were of the hydraulic type and a winch was fitted. The FV1601 was given cargo bodywork with a canvas tilt and it remained in production until 1956.

Example Preserved.

WBH611J	1952	Cargo Truck	Brit. Army	Private Owner

HUMBER FV1604A

Fully restored and looking original in every detail is PCG900G, a Humber FV1604A with radio bodywork.

(C. Pearce)

The Humber FV1604A was a 1-ton normal control 4 × 4 model, first introduced in 1952. Having a wheelbase of 9 ft. 0 in. it was given a Rolls Royce 6-cylinder petrol engine of 4256 cc. and had a 5-speed gearbox with 2-speed transfer box. Its brakes were hydraulically operated. Wireless bodywork was fitted and the FV1604A remained in production until 1956.

Examples Preserved.

SPN249	1953	Wireless	Brit. Army	Mitchell, Upper Hartfield
PCG900G	1955	Wireless	Brit. Army	Pearce, Titchfield

HUMBER FV1621

Immaculately restored is GGR653S, a Humber FV1621 missile supply vehicle.

(K. A. Jenkinson)

Built at Rootes' Maidstone factory, the Humber FV1621 was first introduced in 1952, being a 1-ton 4×4 vehicle of normal control layout with a wheelbase of 9 ft. 0 in. It was given a Rolls Royce B60-type 6-cylinder petrol engine of 4.25 litres capacity and had a 5-speed gearbox with single speed transfer box and power take off. Hydraulic brakes were fitted. The FV1621 was built as a missile supply vehicle for carrying missiles prior to launching. The example preserved was built as an FV1601 general service truck and was rebodied to FV1621 specification in 1960 for the Malkara Missile Project.

Example Preserved.

GGR653S   1955   Missile Supply   Brit. Army   Foster, Birtley

HUMBER FV1611/FV1620

Known as the Humber Pig, the FV1611 was a 4 × 4 armoured vehicle, an example of which-05BF71 is depicted here.

(D. Game)

The Humber FV1611, generally known as the 'Humber Pig' was first built in 1952. The FV1611, based on the FV1600 series 1-ton truck, was an armoured 4 × 4 vehicle of normal control configuration and was powered by a Rolls Royce 6-cylinder B60 Mk.5A petrol engine. It had a 5-speed gearbox and used a wheelbase of 9 ft. 0 in. Bodywork was built by Sankeys and the ROF and the 'Pig' remained in production until 1961. The FV1620 was basically an FV1611 mounted with a twin launcher at the rear of the hull for 2 Malkara wire-guided missiles. Introduced in 1955, it too remained in production until 1961.

Examples Preserved.

FV1611			APC	Brit. Army	Warnham War Museum
FV1611	05BF71		APC	Brit. Army	Imperial War Museum Duxford
FV1611			APC	Brit. Army	Goodman, Bourne
FV1611			APC	Brit. Army	Wilkinson, St. Albans
FV1611			APC	Brit. Army	Wilson, Kent
FV1611	PNM935J	1952	APC	Brit. Army	Haynes, Wednesbury
FV1611		1954	APC	Brit. Army	Elvis, Water Orton
		1956	APC	Brit. Army	Peters, Portland
FV1613		1954	Ambulance	Brit. Army	Peters, Portland
FV1620	06BK66	1960	Missile Launcher	Brit. Army	RAC Museum, Bovington

HUMBER HEXONAUT

The Humber Hexonaut, introduced during the early part of World War II was a 15 cwt. 6×6 truck. Powered by 2 Hillman 14 hp. engines and transmission units, each driving the wheels on one side of the vehicle, the Hexonaut could float and was designed to be carried in Dakota aircraft. Skid steering was applied by levers operating throttles and brakes. Only 3 Hexonauts were ever built.

Example Preserved.

Amphibian	Brit. Army	Warnham War Museum

HUMBER Mk.I ARMOURED CAR

The Humber Mk.I armoured scout car had a comparatively short production life before being superceded by the Mk.II. This official view of a Mk.I was taken before its armaments were fitted.
(Chrysler Ltd.)

The Humber Mk.I armoured car entered production in 1941. It could be used as a 4×2 or 4×4 vehicle by the operation of a shift lever and it was powered by a Humber 6-cylinder petrol engine as used in the Super Snipe car. Numerous Commer mechanical components were incorporated and it was armed with 1×15 mm. Besa MG and 1×7.92 mm. Besa MG. The Mk.I was superceded by the Mk.II and Mk.III in 1942.

Examples Preserved.

1941	Scout Car	Brit. Army	RAC Museum, Bovington
1942	Scout Car	Brit. Army	Busby, Hook Norton
1942	Scout Car	Brit. Army	Marchant, Milton Keynes
1942	Scout Car	Brit. Army	Thomas, London

INTERNATIONAL 1853FC

Introduced in 1962, the International 1853FC was a 4×2 forward control bus cum ambulance. Having a wheelbase of 17 ft. 4 in. it was fitted with an International 6-cylinder petrol engine of 7388 cc. and had a 5-speed gearbox and full air brakes. When used as a bus, it had seating for 44 passengers. The 1853FC remained in production until 1966.

Example Preserved.

YWP494M	1964	Bus	US Air Force	Barker, Cirencester

INTERNATIONAL K7

Introduced in 1941, the International K7 is a normal control 2½-ton 4×2 model with a wheelbase of 13 ft. 2 in., although other wheelbase measurements were available. Being a civilian model modified only in detail to satisfy military requirements, it was powered by an International 6-cylinder petrol engine of 101 bhp. and had a 5-speed gearbox. 7,498 were built for military purposes and various types of bodywork fitted included cargo, derrick, dump and bus. Production of the military K7 ended in 1943.

Example Preserved.

GGU34	1941	Tipper	Brindley, Wolverhampton

INTERNATIONAL M5A1

The International M5A1 was introduced in 1942 as a half-track personnel carrier of normal control layout. Having a wheelbase of 11 ft. 3½ in. it was powered by an International 6-cylinder petrol engine of 143 bhp. and used a 4-speed gearbox with 2-speed transfer box. It had a welded hull and was fitted with a ring mount, and carried a crew of 13. It remained in production until 1945.

Examples Preserved.

52YZ78	1942	APC	US Army	SEME, Bordon
	1942	APC	US Army	Wilkinson, St. Albans
	1942	APC		Jones, Salop
	1942	APC		Hichman, Worcs.
	1942	APC		Lamb, Thatcham
	1943	APC		Chapman, Kettering
	1943	APC	Brit. Army	RAC Museum, Bovington
	1943	APC	US Army	Mann, Lamanva
	1944	APC	US Army	Anderson, Otterburn

INTERNATIONAL M9A1

This International M9A1 dating from 1943 is equipped as a tank recovery vehicle.

(K. A. Jenkinson)

The International M9A1 was a half-track car built to carry a crew of 10. First produced in 1941, the M9A1, was outwardly and technically similar to the M5A1, having a wheelbase of 11 ft. 3½ in. and being powered by an International 6-cylinder petrol engine of 143 bhp. with a 4-speed gearbox and 2-speed transfer box. 1,419 were supplied to the UK where they were all converted to M5A1 specification before entering service. The M9A1 remained in production until 1944.

Examples Preserved.

	1942	APC	Brit. Army	Anderson, Otterburn
FUF53	1943	Tank Recovery	Brit. Army	Warnham War Museum
MUH454P	1943	APC		Milton, Pontypridd

JAGDPANTHER Sd Kfz 173

First produced in 1943, the Jagdpanther was a self-propelled mounting consisting of an 8.8 cm. gun mounted in the front plate of a turretless version of the Panther tank. It additionally was mounted with 1 × MG and was driven by a Maybach 700 bhp. engine. Of 22 ft. 7 in. length, 10 ft. 9 in. width and 8 ft. 11 in. height, it accommodated a crew of five. 230 Jagdpanthers were built before this model was discontinued in 1944.

Examples Preserved.

	1944	S.P. Gun	Ger. Army	RAC Museum, Bovington
	1944		Ger. Army	Imperial War Museum, Duxford

JAGDPANTHER 38(t), HETZER (BAITER)

The 38(t) Hetzer first appeared in 1944, being a self-propelled mounting consisting of 1 × 7.5 cm. gun and 1 × MG mounted onto a Czechoslovakian Skoda tank chassis. Its forward mounted Praga engine was a 150 hp. unit and the Hetzer was a well armoured, low-built vehicle capable of speeds up to 25 mph. It was 16 ft. 0 in. long, 8 ft. 8 in. wide and 6 ft. 11 in. high with accommodation for a crew of 4. Production took place only in 1944 during which time a total of 1,577 were built.

Example Preserved.

        1944 S.P. Gun   Germ. Army RAC Museum, Bovington

JAGDTIGER

The huge Jagdtiger was the most powerfully armed fighting vehicle to enter service in World War II. Only 48 were ever built, and this one is the sole survivor today.

(K. A. Jenkinson)

Built by Henschel, the Jagdtiger was the most powerfully armed fighting vehicle to enter service in World War II. Being a self-propelled 12.8 cm. gun, with 1 × MG, it was mounted on a Tiger II with fixed superstructure. It was 25 ft. 7 in. long, 11 ft. 11 in. wide and 9 ft. 3 in. high and was powered by a Maybach 700 bhp. engine. Only 48 were built, all being constructed during 1944.

Example Preserved.

        1944 S.P. Gun   Germ. Army RAC Museum, Bovington

KRUPP L2H143

Using an unusual frontal appearance, the design of the Krupp L2H is illustrated here with preserved JPF878N.

(C. Pearce)

The German built Krupp L2H143 was a light 6×4 model of normal control design with a wheelbase of 2,900 mm. Introduced in 1933, it had a Krupp 4-cylinder petrol engine and 4-speed gearbox with a 2-speed transfer box, the brakes being hydraulically operated. Numerous types of bodywork were fitted and the L2H143 was discontinued in 1937 when it was superseded by the much advanced L2H43 model.

Example Preserved.

L2H43 JPF878N 1940 Troop Carrier   Germ. Army Oliver, Eton Wick

KV IB

The Russian KV IB was based upon the KV I which had first appeared in September 1939. It had a centrally mounted turret containing a 76.2 mm. gun and two machine guns, one of which was co-axial and had exceptionally wide tracks. Its rear mounted engine was a 550 hp. 12-cylinder V-2K diesel unit and the KV IB could carry a crew of 5. Heavily armoured, it was 22 ft. 3½ in. long, 10 ft. 11½ in. wide and 10 ft. 8 in. high.

Example Preserved.

        1940 Tank   Russian   RAC Museum, Bovington
                            Army

LANCHESTER

Built in the 'between wars' period, the Lanchester armoured car was specifically designed for this purpose. MT9755 shown here has now been fully restored.

(K. A. Jenkinson)

The Lanchester was the first armoured car in British service to have been specifically designed as such. First produced in 1928, the chassis used was a 6-wheeler with both rear axles being driven. The engine used was a Lanchester 6-cylinder unit of 88 bhp. and the vehicle was armed with $1 \times .5$ in. Vickers MG and $1 \times .303$ cal. Vickers MG in its turret whilst some vehicles were also equipped with $1 \times .303$ cal. MG in the hull. The Mk.I had twin rear wheels whilst the Mk.II was fitted with single rear wheels. An interesting feature of the Lanchester was that a duplicate steering wheel and linkage was fitted at the rear of the crew compartment facing backwards. Only 39 of these armoured cars were built before production ceased in 1932.

Example Preserved.

Mk.II MT9755   1931   Armoured Car   Brit. Army   RAC Museum, Bovington

LANDROVER

The Land Rover has seen wide use with the British Military Forces. This broadside view shows XAA129 complete with canvas tilt.

Formally launched in 1948, the Land Rover has since its inception been widely used by the armed forces and is a very versatile 4×4 vehicle. Originally introduced with a wheelbase of 6 ft. 8 in., it was powered by a Rover 4-cylinder petrol engine of 1.59 litres capacity. Transmission was via a 4-speed gearbox (the vehicle having permanent 4-wheel drive) whilst the brakes were hydraulically operated, acting on all 4 wheels. In 1950 a new 4-speed gearbox with 2-speed transfer box replaced the original gearbox to give optional 2- or 4-wheel drive. Two years later, the original engine was superseded by a more powerful 1.99 litre 4-cylinder Rover petrol unit and in 1954 its wheelbase was increased to 7 ft. 2 in. In 1956 the series II Land Rover replaced the earlier model. This had a wheelbase of 7 ft. 4 in. but retained the same mechanical components as the previous model. In addition, a longer version was introduced in 1956, this having a wheelbase of 9 ft. 1 in. In addition to being used as a utility vehicle, the long wheelbase model was also fitted with ambulance bodywork. Whilst the 9 ft. 1 in. model is still in production, the short wheelbase version was phased out during the late 'sixties when it was replaced by a new model.

Examples Preserved.

CPO854B	1950	Utility		Beddall, Iver
OBH168	1951	Utility		Beddall, Iver
272WMB	1951	Utility	Brit. Army	Hallett, Tarporley
		Utility		Dodds, Hexham
	1952	Utility		Peters, Bridport
LKD669	1952	Utility		Bedall, Iver
XAA129		Utility		
		Utility		Sellers, Middlesbrough
		Utility		Smith, Newcastle upon Tyne
	1957	Utility		Hermes, Buckfastleigh

LEOPARD I

Bearing German Army markings, this preserved Leopard I dates from 1961.

(K. A. Jenkinson)

The Leopard I main battle tank first entered production in 1965, a few proto-types having been completed some years prior to this. Built in Germany, it is powered by an MTU 10-cylinder multi-fuel engine and is 23 ft. 3 in. long, 10 ft. 8 in. wide and 8 ft. 8 in. high. It is armed with 1×105 mm. gun (ironically pro-duced in England), and 1×7.62 mm. co-axial MG with 1×7.62 mm. MG mounted on its roof and 4 smoke dischargers on each side of its turret. Numerous variants have been produced for special purposes and the Leopard I is still being built.

Example Preserved.

1961 Tank   Germ. Army RAC Museum, Bovington

110

LEYLAND HIPPO Mk.II

Many of the wartime Leyland Hippo Mk.II lorries remained in use with the British Army into the 'seventies. One of those now preserved is TVE867S, seen here after being completely restored.

(K. A. Jenkinson)

The Leyland Hippo Mk.II, introduced in 1944, was a 6 × 4, 10-ton GS vehicle of forward control layout. It was powered by a Leyland 6-cylinder 7.4 litre diesel engine and was given a 5-speed gearbox with 2-speed transfer box. It had a wheelbase of 15 ft. 6 in. and carried GS bodywork. In 1945 a number were constructed with van bodywork and the Hippo Mk.II remained in production until 1946.

Examples Preserved.

	1944	G/S Lorry	Brit. Army	Gliddon, Carshalton
64YY29	1944	G/S Lorry	Brit. Army	Bowman, Blaydon
TVE867S	1944	G/S Lorry	Brit. Army	Webb & Seabrook, Duxford
	1944	G/S Lorry	Brit. Army	NWTM, Burtonwood
2425768	1945	G/S Lorry	Brit. Army	Beddows, Northants
MJK372	1945	G/S Lorry	Brit. Army	Shone, London
	1945	G/S Lorry	Brit. Army	RCT, Aldershot
	1945	G/S Lorry	Brit. Army	Stallwood, London
53YY92	1946	G/S Lorry	Brit. Army	Dean, Paisley
	1944	G/S Lorry	Brit. Army	Lane, Ripley, Derbys

LEYLAND HIPPO Mk.III

The Leyland 19H/1 Hippo Mk.III was introduced in 1952 as a 10-ton 6×4 vehicle of forward control layout. Given a Leyland 0.600 6-cylinder diesel engine, the Hippo Mk.III had a wheelbase of 15 ft. 6 in. Transmission was via a 5-speed gearbox with 2-speed transfer box. Used mainly by the RAF., various types of body could be fitted including radar and glider winch, The Hippo Mk.III continued in production until the late 'fifties.

Example Preserved.

| 1955 | Radar | RAF | RAF Museum, Henlow |

LEYLAND LYNX WDZ1

JTT724, a Leyland Lynx cargo truck of 1940 vintage is shown whilst awaiting restoration.

(K. A. Jenkinson)

The WDZ1 was a military version of the civilian Leyland Lynx introduced in 1937. Of semi-forward control, the WDZ1 was put into production in 1940 and had a wheelbase of 12 ft. 0 in. It was powered by a Leyland 6-cylinder petrol engine of 29.4 hp and had a 5-speed gearbox, single dry plate clutch and hydraulic brakes. Designed as a 4×2, 3-ton truck, it was built at Leyland's Kingston upon Thames factory and remained in production until the latter part of 1941.

Example Preserved.

| JTT724 | 1940 | Cargo | Hoare, Chepstow |

LEYLAND MARTIAN

Introduced in 1950, the Leyland Martian was a 10-ton 6×6 vehicle of normal control layout. Having a wheelbase of 14 ft. 6 in. it was powered by a Rolls Royce B81-type 8-cylinder engine of 215 bhp. and had a 4-speed gearbox with 3-speed transfer box. Air brakes were fitted. The Martian was used with artillery tractor (FV1103) or heavy recovery (FV1119) bodywork and was additionally built with 17 ft. 9 in. wheelbase for use as a cargo truck (FV1110A).

Example Preserved.

FV1103	1952	Artillery Tractor	Brit. Army	McIntyre, Birchington

LEYLAND RETRIEVER WLW1

A typical Leyland Retriever WLW1 cargo truck seen here in post-war civilian use.
(K. A. Jenkinson collection)

The Leyland Retriever was introduced in 1939 and was a 3 ton 6×4 model of forward control layout. Having a wheelbase of 13 ft. 0 in. it was powered by a Leyland 4-cylinder petrol engine rated at 33.3 hp. and had a 4-speed gearbox with 2-speed transfer box and vacuum assisted hydraulic brakes. Various types of bodywork could be fitted including GS, machinery, breakdown, workshop, derrick, bridging, gun mounts, wireless and Coles crane. The Retriever continued in production until 1943.

Examples Preserved.

	1939	Workshop		Brindley, Wolverhampton
01XY39	1939	Caravan	Brit. Army	Imperial War Museum, London
	1940	Wrecker		Hoare, Chepstow
	1940	Crane		Mason, Ipswich

LEYLAND TERRIER TSE4

ZD3482, a Leyland Terrier cargo truck now safely preserved in Ireland.

(M. Corcoran)

The Leyland Terrier TSE4 introduced in 1937 was a 3-ton 6×4 vehicle of forward control layout. Fitted with a Leyland 4-cylinder petrol engine and 4-speed gearbox, it had hydraulic brakes. Equipped with a winch, it was used as a cargo carrier and for towing anti-aircraft artillery. The Terrier remained in production until 1940.

Example Preserved.

ZD3482   1939 G/S Truck   TMI, Castleruddery

LIGHT TANK Mk.II

Fully restored MT9742, a 1931 Light Tank Mk.II.

(K. A. Jenkinson)

The Light Tank Mk.II was a production development of the 'private venture' Carden-Loyd tanks supplied to the War Office in 1929. Built by Vickers for the British army, the Mk.II was put into full production in 1931 being 11 ft. 9 in. in length, 6 ft. 3½ in. wide and 6 ft. 7½ in. high. Armed with 1 × Vickers .303 MG, the Mk.II was powered by a Rolls Royce 6-cylinder 66 hp. petrol engine. Built to carry a crew of 2, the Mk.II was discontinued in 1936.

Example Preserved.

MT9742	1931	Tank	Brit. Army	RAC Museum, Bovington

LIGHT TANK Mk.IV

The Light Tank Mk.IV is illustrated here in the form of BMM121.

(K. A. Jenkinson)

The Light Tank Mk.IV was first introduced in 1932 for the British Army. It differed from the Mk.I-III by having no separate rear idler wheel and was more powerful than the previous Light Tanks. Powered by a Meadows 88 hp. 6-cylinder petrol engine it was 11 ft. 2 in. long, 6 ft. 11½ in. wide and 6 ft. 8½ in. high. It was armed with 1 × Vickers .303 MG or 1 × .5 in. Vickers MG and it remained in production until 1936.

Example Preserved.

BMM121	1935	Tank	Brit. Army	RAC Museum, Bovington

LIGHT TANK Mk.VIB

Safely preserved for the benefit of future generations is HMC547, a British Army Light Tank Mk.VIB dating from 1938.

(K. A. Jenkinson)

Built for both the British and Indian armies, the Light Tank Mk.VIB was a development of the Mk.VI introduced in 1936. Powered by a Meadows 6-cylinder 88 hp. petrol engine, the VIB differed from the VI by having a round instead of multi-sided turret cupola. It was 12 ft. 11½ in. long, 6 ft. 9 in. wide and 7 ft. 3½ in. high and was armed with a main armament of 1 × Vickers .5 in. MG and 1 × 15 mm. Besa MG. The Mk. VIB remained in production until 1940.

Example Preserved.

HMC547	1938	Tank	Brit. Army	RAC Museum, Bovington

LITTLE WILLIE

Built in 1915 for British Army use in World War I was Little Willie.

(K. A. Jenkinson)

Fosters of Lincoln started to build a prototype armoured vehicle in August 1915 using boiler plate instead of armour plate. Fitted with Bullock tracks, it had a pair of wheels behind to aid steering and improve the balance. Redesigned in December 1915, it was then given the name 'Little Willie'. Having an overall length of 26 ft. 6 in. it was fitted with a 6-cylinder 105 hp. Foster-Daimler engine as used in the pre-World War I tractor bearing that name. It performed well on its trials but was never put into production, being superceded by another design known as 'Big Willie' which was nearing completion.

Example Preserved.

| 1915 | Tank | Brit. Army | RAC Museum, Bovington |

LOCOMOBILE

Introduced in 1914, the Locomobile was a 3½-ton truck with a wheelbase of 12 ft. 6 in. It was powered by a 28.9 hp. 4-cylinder engine and had a 4-speed gearbox and worm driven rear axle. Solid tyres were fitted. Used by both the US and British Armies, the latter had 1,192 in service when production ended in 1918.

Example Preserved.

| XK548 | 1914 | Cargo | Brit. Army | Webb, Sudbury |

LOCUST

T158979, the preserved Locust light airborne tank.

(K. A. Jenkinson)

The American built M22 Light Tank (Airborne) was given the name Locust when in British service. Based on a design drawn up in 1941, the first Locusts were shipped to England for evaluation in 1943. Carried by Hamilcar gliders, a number were used up until 1945. Powered by a Lycoming 0-435T 6-cylinder 162 hp. petrol engine, the Locust was armed with 1 × 37 mm. M6 gun and 1 × .30 cal. Browning MG and was 12 ft. 11 in. long, 7 ft. 1 in. wide and 6 ft. 1 in. high.

Example Preserved.

T158979	1942	Tank	Brit. Army	RAC Museum, Bovington

LOYD CARRIER

T258486, restored to complete originality is a Loyd Carrier.

(P. Isaac)

First produced in 1939 the Loyd Carrier was initially designed as a personnel carrier, being a tracked vehicle based on the Fordson 4×2, 15 cwt. truck. Powered by a Ford V8 30 hp. petrol engine and having a 4-speed gearbox, the radiator was mounted at the rear whilst the drive was taken to the front driving sprockets. The brakes were originally of the Bendix type but later these were changed to Girling hydraulics. The hull was of a simple open top design and was unarmoured although light armour plates could be fitted if required. At first the Loyd Carrier was built solely by Vivian Loyd & Co. Ltd., but after 1941 it was also built by Sentinel, Aveling-Barford, Dennis, Wolseley and Ford, production continuing throughout World War II.

Examples Preserved.

T136112	Carrier	Brit. Army	Imperial War Museum, Duxford
	Carrier	Brit. Army	Mankin, Heddon on the Wall
T258486	Carrier	Brit. Army	Isaac, Umberleigh

This rear view of a preserved M40 self-propelled gun clearly illustrates its opening rear portion.

(K. A. Jenkinson)

The M40 self-propelled gun, often referred to as 'Long Tom' was introduced in March 1945. Mounted on a modified M4 Sherman chassis and powered by a Continental 9-cylinder radial air-cooled petrol engine, its armament consisted of a 155 mm. M2 gun. Carrying a crew of 8, it was 29 ft. 7 in. long, 10 ft. 4 in. wide and 8 ft. 9 in. high. It remained in production until the end of 1945.

Example Preserved.

93BA48	1945	S.P. Gun	Brit. Army	Imperial War Museum, London

The now preserved Patton M47 medium tank.

(K. A. Jenkinson)

The M47 medium tank made its debut in 1952, being produced by the Detroit Tank Arsenal and the American Locomotive Co. Armed with 1 × 90 mm. gun and 1 × .3 in. co-axial MG, 1 × 3 in. MG in the bow and 1 × .5 in. MG. on the commander's cupola, the M47 was the last American tank to have a bow-mounted MG. Designed to carry a crew of 5, it was 20 ft. 10¾ in. long, 10 ft. 6 in. wide and 11 ft. 0 in. high. It was powered by a Continental AV-1790-5B 12-cylinder air cooled petrol engine and was fitted with infra-red driving lights. Known also as the Patton, I, the M47 was superceded by the M48 in 1952/53.

Example Preserved.

1952	Tank	US Army	RAC Museum, Bovington

M48

9A5213, an American built M48 tank produced during the post-war period.

Production of the M48 began in 1952 following design work by Chrysler. Being an American medium tank, the M48 was in fact not built by its designers, but by Ford, the Fisher Body Division of GMC and Alco Products. Chrysler did however gain a production order in 1959. Armed with 1 × 90 mm. gun and 1 × .3 in. co-axial MG with 1 × .5 in. MG in the commander's cupola, the M48 was powered by a Continental AVDS-1790-2A 12-cylinder air cooled diesel engine. It had infra-red driving lights and some were given an infra-red/white searchlight mounted over the main armament. It was 22 ft. 7 in. long, 11 ft. 11 in. wide and 10 ft. 3 in. high and during its years of production was updated in a number of ways, finally being discontinued in 1960.

Example Preserved.

| 9A5213 | 1952 | Tank | US Army | RAC Museum, Bovington |

M59

The M59 was used as an armoured personnel carrier during the mid 'fifties.

(K. A. Jenkinson)

Built by FMC in California, the M59 armoured personnel carrier was put into full production in 1954 following the successful testing of a few prototypes. Powered by 2 GMC 302 6-cylinder petrol engines, it was designed to carry a crew of 2 plus 10 other personnel. It was armed with 1 × 12.7 mm. MG and remained in production until 1959.

Example Preserved.

1952   Personnel Carrier   US Army   RAC Museum, Bovington

M113

The M113 armoured personnel carrier was a fully tracked vehicle built by FMC in California. Introduced in 1960, it is powered by a GMC 6-cylinder diesel engine and is armed with 1 × 12.7 mm. Browning MG. It is 15 ft. 11 in. long, 8 ft. 10 in. wide and 8 ft. 2 in. high and carries a crew of 2 with additional accommodation for 11 troops. The M113 is fully amphibious and is fitted with infra-red night driving lights. Its construction is all aluminium and there are more variants than any other fighting vehicle in service today. In addition to being produced in America, the M113 is also built by Oto Melara in Italy and to date more than 64,000 have been produced. The M113 still remains in production today.

Example Preserved.

OODC51   1964   Personnel Carrier   Brit. Army   RAC Museum, Bovington

124

MACK NM5

This Mack NM5, numbered J9052 is now preserved in Jersey.

(HCVS Collection)

The Mack NM5 was a 6-ton 6×6 vehicle of normal control layout. First produced in 1941, it was powered by a Mack 6-cylinder petrol engine of 159 bhp., and had a 5-speed gearbox and 2-speed transfer box. It had a wheelbase of 14 ft. 9 in. and had hydraulically operated brakes. The NM5 was used extensively for Lend-Lease requirements and was fitted with cargo bodywork. It remained in production until 1945.

Example Preserved.

J9052	1943	G/S Truck	Brit. Army	O'Donoghue, St. Peter, Jersey

MACK NO2

Looking massive when compared with the Austin K2 standing behind it, this Mack NO2 Prime Mover is restored to its original U.S. Army specification.

(K. A. Jenkinson)

The Mack NO2 was introduced in 1940 and was a 6×6, seven and a half ton model of normal control layout. It had a wheelbase of 13 ft. 0 in. and was fitted with a Mack 6-cylinder EY type petrol engine of 159 bhp. Transmission was via a 5-speed gearbox with 2-speed transfer box and air brakes were fitted, plus controls for electric trailer brakes. Classified as a Prime Mover, the NO2 was unusual in that it had a double reduction gear in the steering ends of the driven front axle, the steering ends being of a type in which bevel gears concentric with the king pins drove the wheels and allowed for steering, thereby dispensing with universal joints. This resulted in the axle being higher that the wheel hubs, thus providing extra ground clearance. The NO2 remained in production until 1945.

Example Preserved.

KPT313T   1942   Prime Mover   Newton, Bishop Auckland

MACK NR6

First produced in 1941, the Mack NR6 was a 10-ton 6×4 normal control model with a wheelbase of 16 ft. 8½ in. Powered by a Mack-Lanova 6-cylinder diesel engine of 131 bhp. it had a 5-speed gearbox with 2-speed transfer box and was fitted with air brakes. Cargo bodywork was fitted and the NR6 remained in production until 1945.

Example Preserved.

59XE34   1941   Caravan   Brit. Army   Imperial War Museum,
London

MARMON-HERRINGTON IV

The Marmon-Herrington IV was built in South Africa as an armoured car. Having a wheelbase of 9 ft. 10 in. it was a chassis-less vehicle, all its components being attached direct to its all-welded armoured hull. Its rear mounted engine was a Ford 95 bhp. unit whilst the armament carried consisted of 1 × 2 pdr. gun and 1 × .30 cal. Browning MG. Introduced in 1943, the Mk.IV remained in production until 1944.

Example Preserved.

U53350   1942   RAC Museum, Bovington

MARMON HERRINGTON Mk.VI

The Marmon Herrington Mk.VI armoured car was designed for operations in North Africa. Built in South Africa, it was an 8 × 8 vehicle powered by two Ford 8-cylinder petrol engines at the rear of the hull. The first prototype, built in 1943 was armed with 1 × 2 pdr. gun and 1 × Browning .3 in. co-axial MG with 2 × .3 in. MG (AA) on the turret. The second prototype, also built in 1943, was armed with 1 × 6 pdr. gun and 1 × Besa co-axial MG with 1 × .5 in. Browning MG (AA) mounted on its roof. Although large orders where placed for the Mk.VI, these were cancelled before production commenced and no further examples were built.

Example Preserved.

1943   Armoured Car   RAC Museum, Bovington

MATILDA I

Built in 1938, PMX466 is a Matilda I seen here with authentic British Army markings.

(K. A. Jenkinson)

Designated Infantry Tank Mk.I A11, the Matilda I prototype was delivered to the army for trials in September 1936. To keep costs to a minimum, Vickers used a commercial Ford V8 engine and transmission together with many other components adapted from types already used in Vickers light tanks. Full production of the Matilda I commenced in April 1937 and continued until August 1940 by which time a total of 140 (including the pilot model) had been built. Being built for a crew of 2, this model was 15 ft. 11 in. long, 7 ft. 6 in. wide and 6 ft. 1½ in. high. Powered by a Ford V8 70 hp. engine, it was armed with 1 × .5 cal. Vickers MG or 1 × .303 cal. Vickers MG and was of all riveted construction with a cast turret.

Example Preserved.

PMX466   1938   Tank   Brit. Army   RAC Museum, Bovington

MATILDA II

Three Matilda II tanks have survived into preservation, one of which is seen here.

(K. A. Jenkinson)

The Matilda II (Infantry Tank Mk.II A12) was based on the design used for the A7 medium tank which had been designed and built only in prototype form in 1932. The pilot A12 was constructed by Vulcan Foundry of Warrington in 1938 and by the time general production had commenced in June 1938, Fowler and Ruston & Hornsby had been contracted to build the Matilda II under Vulcan's 'parentage'. Some months later, LMS, North British Locomotive and Harland & Wolff were also given contracts, with a total of 2, 987 being built up to August 1943 when the model ceased. Originally, the Matilda II was fitted with twin AEC diesel engines of 87 hp. each, but after 1940 these were joined by twin Leyland 6-cylinder engines of 95 hp. each. The armament mounted consisted of 1×2 pdr. OQF with secondary 1×7.92 cal. Besa MG and this model was easily distinguished by its heavy armoured side skirts which concealed its suspension. It had a length of 18 ft. 5 in., width of 8 ft. 6 in. and height of 8 ft. 3 in. Numerous variants were produced, one of which was the Matilda II CDL (canal defense light). This was an armoured housing with powerful searchlight fitted in place of the tank's original turret for use in illuminating battlefields in night actions.

Examples Preserved.

	T6875		Tank	Brit. Army	Imperial War Museum, London
	T10459	1939		Brit. Army	RAC Museum, Bovington
CDL	T7341	1943		Brit. Army	RAC Museum, Bovington

MERCEDES-BENZ UNIMOG

Used by the German Army, this Mercedes Benz Unimog of 1960 vintage is fitted with radio bodywork.

(S. Levee)

The Mercedes-Benz Unimog first appeared in 1948 designed as a 4×4 multi-purpose vehicle for agricultural and industrial use. During the following year it made its debut as a military vehicle and from then until the mid sixties it was built in a variety of forms. Being a 1-1½-ton 4×4 vehicle of semi-forward control layout, it was available with 1.72 m., 2.20 m. or 2.90 m. wheelbase and could be fitted with either a Daimler-Benz 6-cylinder oil engine or a 6-cylinder petrol unit. It had a 6-speed gearbox with 2-speed transfer box and front and rear diff locks and was equipped with hydraulic brakes. A variety of bodywork could be fitted including truck, radio, house type van or ambulance, and the Unimog was used by the West German military services and the armies of Austria, France, Britain and Belgium.

Examples Preserved.

Y-392-842	1960	Radio	Germ. Army	Private Owner
		Ambulance	Germ. Army	Pearce Smith, Lyndhurst

MORRIS LIGHT RECONNAISSANCE

2,200 of these Morris Light Reconnaissance vehicles were built during World War II.

(K. A. Jenkinson)

Introduced in 1941, the Morris Light Reconnaissance was an armoured vehicle of 4×2 configuration. Powered by a Morris 4-cylinder petrol engine of 71 bhp., it has a 4-speed gearbox and was armed with 1×0.0303 in. light Bren machine gun and 1×Boys anti-tank rifle. Its engine was at the rear and in 1942 the Mk.II was introduced, this being a 4×4 model. Two thousand two hundred Morris Light Reconnaissance vehicles were built before production ended in 1944.

Example Preserved.

1941   Reconnaissance   Brit. Army   RAC Museum, Bovington

MORRIS M

Typical of the Morris M type, this RAF example was fitted with ambulance bodywork.

The Morris M was a normal control light utility of 4 × 2 configuration. Having a wheelbase of 7 ft. 10 in. it was fitted with a 10 hp. 4-cylinder petrol engine, 4-speed gearbox and hydraulic brakes. Some M-types were fitted with the smaller Morris 8 hp. 4-cylinder petrol engine. Introduced in 1939, the M continued in production until 1944.

Examples Preserved.

LGV523	1940	Utility		Private Owner
JHV515	1941	Ambulance	RAF	Private Owner

MORRIS COMMERCIAL C4

Replacing the CS8 in 1944, the Morris Commercial C4 was built with two different wheelbase measurements. The Mk.I had a wheelbase of 8 ft. 2 in. whilst the Mk.II and Mk.III had a measurement of 8 ft. 11 in. Of normal control layout, the C4 was powered by a Morris 4-cylinder 24.8 hp. petrol engine with a bore and stroke of 100 mm. × 112 mm. It was given a 4-speed gearbox, single dry plate clutch and fully floating spiral bevel rear axle whilst its brakes were hydraulically operated and acted on all 4-wheels. Available with various bodywork, the C4 was discontinued in 1945.

Example Preserved.

KKN983	1944	G/S Cargo	Brit. Army	MT Preservation Group, Croydon

MORRIS COMMERCIAL C8

UJT584, a Morris Commercial C8 shown after being fully restored to its original specification.

(C. Juggler)

Introduced towards the end of 1938, the Morris Commercial C8 was a 15 cwt. 4 × 4 model of normal control layout often known as the Quad. It had an 8 ft. 3 in. wheelbase and was powered by a Morris 3.5 litre 4-cylinder petrol engine with a bore and stroke of 100 mm. × 112 mm. A 5-speed gearbox was fitted with single dry plate clutch whilst the rear axle was of the spiral bevel type. Hydraulic brakes acted on all 4-wheels. The C8 was fitted with general service bodywork and remained in production until 1945.

Examples Preserved.

	1938	Artillery Tractor	Brit. Army	Pearce, Holywell
SJT395	1939	Artillery Tractor	Brit. Army	Groom, Warlingham
ZD986	1939	Artillery Tractor		TMI, Castleruddery
		G/S Truck	Brit. Army	Langley, Bucks.
		G/S Truck	Brit. Army	Birnie, Herts.
		G/S Truck	Brit. Army	Cleaver, Chaulington
		Artillery Tractor	Brit. Army	Jones, Salop.
WRK995N	1940	Artillery Tractor	Brit. Army	RAC Museum, Bovington
16RD69	1942	Breakdown	Brit. Army	Matthews, Dunton Green
GLN282	1942	Artillery Tractor	Brit. Army	Hallyburton, Aberargie
		G/S Truck	Brit. Army	King, London
		Artillery Tractor	Brit. Army	Fry, Barry
		Artillery Tractor	Brit. Army	Bellhouse, Hants.
	1943	Artillery Tractor	Brit. Army	Robinson, Burton Latimer
H5847782	1944	Artillery Tractor	Brit. Army	Isaac, Umberleigh
PDL651H	1944	Breakdown	Brit. Army	Fisher, Bembridge
PTK446	1944	Artillery Tractor	Brit. Army	Imperial War Museum, Duxford
THR294	1944	Breakdown	Brit. Army	Hayward, Coulsdon
UJT584	1944	G/S Truck	Brit. Army	Macdonald, Solihull

133

Examples Preserved. *(Continued)*

ZD3177	1944	Artillery Tractor	Brit. Army	TMI, Castleruddery
NVW906C	1944	G/S Truck	Brit. Army	Jackson, Wormingford
	1944	G/S Truck	Brit. Army	Bentley, Swanage
104MTT	1944		Brit. Army	Private Owner
129FPA	1944	Breakdown	Brit. Army	Parker, West Croydon
571FUF	1944	G/S Truck	Brit. Army	Sarjantson, Tunbridge Wells
832EPC	1944	G/S Truck	Brit. Army	Deadman, Farnham
	1944	Artillery Tractor	Brit. Army	Poole, Surrey
	1944	G/S Truck	Brit. Army	Cremer, Edinburgh
	1944	Artillery Tractor	Brit. Army	Warnham War Museum
	1944		Brit. Army	Martindale, Newcastle
	1944	Artillery Tractor	Brit. Army	Imperial War Museum, Duxford
	1944	G/S Truck	Brit. Army	Mann, Lamanva
	1944	G/S Truck	Brit. Army	Beddows, Northampton
	1944	G/S Truck	Brit. Army	Woodage, Berks.
357DEL	1944	G/S Truck	Brit. Army	Howse, Woodloes Park

MORRIS COMMERCIAL CDFW

Produced in the pre-World War II period, the Morris Commercial CDFW has a somewhat dated look. This example is 1067CX.

(K. A. Jenkinson)

Introduced in 1933, the Morris Commercial CDFW was a semi-forward control 6×4, 30 cwt. vehicle with a wheelbase of 10 ft. 7½ in. Powered by a Morris Commercial 4-cylinder 55 bhp. petrol engine, it had a 5-speed gearbox and was fitted with a 4-ton winch. In addition to being built as a GS truck and winch, it was also produced as a mobile office. The CDFW remained in production until 1940.

Example Preserved.

1067CX	1935	Personnel Carrier	Brit. Army	Moore, Huddersfield

134

MORRIS COMMERCIAL CDSW

Restored to its original 1940 condition is Morris Commercial CDSW JMX842.

(R. Peacock)

The Morris Commercial CDSW was a 30 cwt. 6×4 model introduced in 1938. Of normal control layout, it had a wheelbase of 9 ft. 7½ in. and was powered by a Morris 6-cylinder 25.01 hp. petrol engine. Transmission was via a 5-speed crash gearbox and dry plate clutch whilst final drive was by means of a worm. The brakes were hydraulically operated, acting on the front and centre wheels. Fitted with artillery tractor bodywork, it was also built as a light recovery vehicle and remained in production until 1944.

Examples Preserved.

	1938	Artillery Tractor	Brit. Army	Pearce, Holywell
HAD130	1939	Artillery Tractor	Brit. Army	Doynton, Bristol
GBW245S	1939	Artillery Tractor	Brit. Army	Houlahan & Busby, Hook Norton
RUB425R	1939	Artillery Tractor	Irish Army	Peacock, Leeds
ZD296	1939	Artillery Tractor	Brit. Army	TMI, Castleruddery
JMX842	1940	Artillery Tractor	Brit. Army	Sales, Surrey
		Artillery Tractor	Brit. Army	Blyth, Holt
	1941	Light Recovery	Brit. Army	Private Owner
	1941	Light Recovery	Brit. Army	Campbell, Chester le Street.

MORRIS COMMERCIAL CS8

Looking just as it did when in use by the British Army is Morris Commercial CS8 WOR485.

The design of the CS8 was evolved by Morris Commercial in 1934. Being a 4 × 2, 15 cwt. model, it had an 8 ft. 2 in. wheelbase and was given a Morris Commercial 6-cylinder petrol engine rated at 28 hp. Transmission was via a 4-speed gearbox whilst the brakes were hydraulically operated. Although the CS8 was built with various types of bodywork, the standard general service body was the most widely fitted. It remained in production until 1944.

Examples Preserved.

FMX179	1937	G/S Truck	Brit. Army	Sales, Marden
		Compressor	Brit. Army	O'Donaghue, Jersey
MDO106	1939	G/S Truck	Brit. Army	Charman, Market Rasen
	1940	G/S Truck	Brit. Army	Mann, Lamanva
FJK445	1940	G/S Truck	Brit. Army	Farnes, Buxted
WOR485	1940	Compressor	Brit. Army	Deadman, Farnham
		G/S Truck	Brit. Army	Arthurs, Durham

MORRIS COMMERCIAL D

Based on the civilian Morris Commercial D-type truck, this example was used for military service in the early years of its life.

(K. A. Jenkinson)

Introduced in 1927, the Morris Commercial D-type is a 6-wheel 30 cwt. model of normal control layout. Having a wheelbase of 10 ft. 2 in., it was powered by a Morris 4-cylinder 15.9 hp. petrol engine and had a 4-speed double reduction gearbox, single dry plate clutch and overhead worm final drive (both axles being driven). In 1931 the D was given a larger 4-cylinder petrol engine rated at 17.92 hp. and in this form it continued in production until 1933.

Examples Preserved.

ML8881	1927	Troop Carrier	Brit. Army	Bowyer, Devizes
PN7695	1929	Troop Carrier	Brit. Army	Budd, Uckfield

MORRIS COMMERCIAL PU8/4

One of only two Morris Commercial PU8/4 trucks preserved, J13091 is now resident in Jersey.
(K. A. Jenkinson)

Introduced in 1940, the Morris Commercial PU8/4 was a normal control 4×4, 8-cwt model with a wheelbase of 8 ft. 0¼ in. Fitted with a Morris Commercial 6-cylinder petrol engine rated at 74 bhp., it had a 4-speed gearbox and hydraulic brakes. Only a limited number were produced and were fitted with personnel/ G/S bodywork, the model being discontinued in 1941.

Examples Preserved.

J31940	1940	G/S Truck	Brit. Army	O'Donoghue, Jersey
	1940	G/S Truck	Brit. Army	Warnham War Museum

MORRIS COMMERCIAL PU Mk.II

Authentically restored in British Army garb is KBB121, a Morris Commercial PU Mk.II built in 1940.

(K. A. Jenkinson)

Introduced in 1936 the Morris PU was an 8 cwt. 4×2 model of normal control layout. It had a wheelbase of 9 ft. 0 in. and was fitted with a Morris 3.48 litre 6-cylinder petrol engine. Transmission was via a 4-speed gearbox whilst the brakes were hydraulically operated acting on all 4 wheels. The PU was more usually fitted with wireless bodywork and remained in production until 1941.

Examples Preserved.

ROT830G	1936	Breakdown	Brit. Army	Cave, Farnham
811FUF	1937	G/S Truck	Brit. Army	Deadman, Farnham
WAA76H	1937	Wireless	Brit. Army	Warnham War Museum
	1938	Wireless	Brit. Army	Wood, Perth
	1938	Wireless	Brit. Army	Maddison, Bucks.
BIJ1716	1939	Wireless	Brit. Army	RCT, Aldershot
	1939	Wireless	Brit. Army	Cremer, Edinburgh
	1939	Wireless	Brit. Army	Mann, Lamanva
XAJ160S	1940	Wireless	Brit. Army	Chapman, Norton
KKB121	1940	G/S Truck	Brit. Army	Arthurs, Durham
WER501G	1940	G/S Truck	Brit. Army	Mayer, Cheshunt
	1941	Wireless	Brit. Army	Palmer, Exmouth
	1941		Brit. Army	Adams, Shrewton

MORRIS COMMERCIAL TX

Although now preserved in civilian colours, this Morris Commercial TX was originally used by the British Army.

(K. A. Jenkinson)

The Morris Commercial TX was introduced in 1927. A 30 cwt. 4×2 model of normal control layout, it was fitted with a Morris 4-cylinder, 15.9 hp. petrol engine, 4-speed gearbox and mechanically operated brakes. Used by the armed forces as a GS vehicle in the main, the TX remained in production until 1933 by which time its original engine had been replaced by a 19.2 hp. 4-cylinder petrol unit and its carrying capacity increased to 45-50 cwt.

Example Preserved.

RA7580   1927   Personnel Carrier   Brit. Army   Pearson, Masham

NSU KETTENKRAFTRAD

This 1942 Kettenkraftrad preserved in the RAC Museum at Bovington was used during World War II by the German Army.

(K. A. Jenkinson)

The German built Sd.Kfz.2, known as the kleines Kettenkraftrad was a motor-cycle tractor of the half-track type. Built by NSU to carry a crew of 3, it was 9 ft. 9 in. long, 3 ft. 3 in. wide and 3 ft. 11 in. high. Powered by an Opel Olympia 4-cylinder petrol engine of 1478 cc., it had a 3-speed gearbox with 2-speed transfer box and mechanically operated brakes. First built in 1940, the Sd.Kfz.2 remained in production until 1944.

Examples Preserved.

1942	Motorcycle Tractor	Germ. Army	RAC Museum, Bovington
	Motorcycle Tractor	Germ. Army	Oliver, Eton Wick
	Motorcycle Tractor	Germ. Army	Mann, Lamanva

OPEL BLITZ

The Opel Blitz 4 × 4 normal control vehicle was first introduced in 1939. Given a wheelbase of 11 ft. 2½ in., this German built truck was powered by an Opel 6-cylinder, 3626 cc. petrol engine and had a 5-speed gearbox and 2-speed transfer box. Its brakes were hydraulically operated and it could be fitted with various types of bodywork. It remained in production until the early part of 1945.

Examples Preserved.

WH681504 1941	G/S Lorry	Germ. Army	Warnham War Museum
	G/S Lorry	Germ. Army	Mann, Lamanva

PANHARD AML

The Panhard AML was put into production in 1961 following a prototype built some two years earlier. This light armoured car powered by a Panhard model 4 HD 4-cylinder petrol engine has a length of 16 ft. 9 in., width of 12 ft. 5 in. and height of 6 ft. 10 in. It is equipped with 1 × 90 mm. gun, 1 × 7.62 mm. co-axial MG and 2 smoke dischargers each side of its turret whilst an optional 7.62 mm. MG can be fitted on its turret roof. Over 3,400 have been built by Panhard whilst a further 1,000 have been built under licence in South Africa where the type is known as the Eland. The AML is still in production.

Example Preserved.

244-0203	1961	RAC Museum, Bovington

142

PANHARD EBR

The French built Panhard EBR armoured car is represented in preservation by 204-0303, seen here.
(K. A. Jenkinson)

The French built Panhard EBR armoured car first entered production in 1951. Being an 8-wheeler, it is of an unusual design, its front and rear wheels being of the conventional rubber tyred type and used for steering (the EBR has two drivers, one at the front, the other at the rear) whilst its centre 4 wheels have steel grousers, these being lowered when travelling across rough country. Originally armed with 1×90 mm. gun and 1×7.5 mm. co-axial MG with 1×7.5 mm. MG in each drivers position, most EBR's were later re-armed with a new 90 mm. gun which fires fin-stabilised heat and HE rounds. The EBR is powered by a Panhard 12-cylinder air-cooled petrol engine and the vehicle is 20 ft. 2 in. long, 7 ft. 11 in. wide and 7 ft. 7 in. high. It remained in production until 1961.

Example Preserved.

204-0303   1954   French Army RAC Museum, Bovington

PANZERKAMPFWAGEN IB

One of a number of German tanks preserved in Britain, this Panzerkampfwagen IB was built in 1937.

(K. A. Jenkinson)

The German Panzerkampfwagen IB was a light tank based upon a design by Krupp on the lines of the British Vickers-Carden-Loyd light tank. A rear mounted Maybach Krupp air cooled engine was used with the crew compartment in the centre of the vehicle. The turret, mounting two machine guns was off-set to the right on the roof of the hull and an extra road wheel was added to each side to carry the lengthened hull made necessary by the large 100 hp. engine. First produced in 1936, it was 14 ft. 6 in. long, 6 ft. 9 in. wide and 5 ft. 7 in. high.

Example Preserved.

1937   Tank   Germ. Army RAC Museum, Bovington

PANZERKAMPFWAGEN II

Dating from 1941 is this German Panzerkampfwagen II tank.

(K. A. Jenkinson)

Built as an interim measure to supplement the PzKpfw I, the Panzerkampf-wagen II first appeared in prototype form in 1935. Built by MAN, it was heavier and better armed than the PzKpfw I and was given a 6.2 litre Maybach engine of 140 hp. Its engine was rear mounted and its suspension consisted of five road wheels on each side, each sprung independently on leaf springs. Built to carry a crew of 3, it was armed with a 20 mm. cannon and one machine gun. It was 15 ft. 7 in. long, 7 ft. 0 in. wide and 6 ft. 6 in. high. It remained in production until 1941 and over 1,000 were built.

Example Preserved.

1941	Tank	Germ. Army	RAC Museum, Bovington

PANZERKAMPFWAGEN III

Restored complete with its German markings is this Panzerkampfwagen III.

(K. A. Jenkinson)

Developed from prototypes tested in 1936/7, the PzKpfw III was put into production in 1938, it being a 15-ton tank powered by a Maybach 230 hp. engine. Built by Daimler-Benz, it carried a crew of 5 and was armed with 1×3.7 cm. gun and $3 \times$ MG, two of which were co-axial. Designated the PzKpfw III, Ausf.A, it was 18 ft. 8 in. long, 9 ft. 3 in. wide and 7 ft. 8 in. high. In 1941 the PzKpfw III, Ausf.J & L were introduced, these being similar to the Ausf.A. but more heavily armed and fitted with a 300 hp. Maybach engine. These were mounted with 1×5 cm. gun and $2 \times$ MG (one turret, one hull) and were 18 ft. 1 in. long, 9 ft. 8 in. wide and 8 ft. 3 in. high. Production of the PzKpfw III ceased in 1942 by which time 5,644 had been built, some of which were special purpose vehicles. The Ausf.N was basically the same as the Ausf.L except that it was armed with a low velocity 7.5 cm. gun.

Example Preserved.

L   1942   Tank   Germ. Army RAC Museum, Bovington

PANZERKAMPFWAGEN IV

Going into production in 1937, the PzKpfw IV, built by Krupp, had eight road wheels on each side sprung on leaf springs. Fitted with a Maybach 320 hp. engine, the PzKpfw IV, Ausf.B was armed with 1 × 7.5 cm. gun and 2 × MG. It was 19 ft. 3 in. long, 9 ft. 4 in. wide and 8 ft. 6 in. high. In 1941, the PzKpfw IV. Ausf.H appeared, powered by a Maybach 300 hp. engine and armed with an improved 7.5 cm. gun and 2 × MG. The Ausf.H was 19 ft. 4 in. long, 10 ft. 8 in. wide and 8ft. 10 in. high and the PzKpfw IV continued in production until 1943.

Example Preserved.

D/H   1942   Tank   Germ. Army RAC Museum, Bovington

PANZERKAMPFWAGEN V, PANTHER

Showing its 3.7 cm. gun is this preserved German PzKfw V Panther tank.

(K. A. Jenkinson)

The Panther, which developed into one of Germany's most successful tanks copied a number of the features used on the Russian T34. Built by MAN, production commenced in November 1942 and the Panther was equipped with a Maybach 650 hp. engine. The Ausf.D was 22 ft. 7 in. long, 11 ft. 3 in. wide and 9 ft. 8 in. high and was armed with 1 × 7.5 cm. gun and 1 × co-axial MG. The Ausf.A was given a more powerful Maybach engine of 700 hp. and whilst retaining the same length and width of the Ausf.D, it was 6 in. higher. Its armament consisted of 1 × 7.5 cm. gun and 2 × MG. The third version of the Panther was the Ausf.G which whilst using the same engine and armament as the Ausf.A, was 22 ft. 7 in. long, 11 ft. 3 in. wide and 9 ft. 10 in. high. Built to accomodate a crew of 5, the Panther remained in production until 1945.

Example Preserved.

                1942   Tank   Germ. Army RAC Museum, Bovington

PANZERKAMPFWAGEN, VI, TIGER I.

Introduced in 1942, the PzKpfw VI, known as the Tiger I was at first known as the Tiger, Ausführung E. Designed and built by Henschel it was over 30-tons in weight and was powered by a Maybach 700 hp. engine. When it first made its debut, it was the most powerful tank in service anywhere in the world and was armed with 1 × 8.8 cm. gun and 2 × MG. It was 20 ft. 4 in. long, 12 ft. 3 in. wide and 9 ft. 5 in. high and 1,350 were built before production ceased in 1944.

Example Preserved.

      1942   Tank   Germ. Army RAC Museum, Bovington

PANZERKAMPFWAGEN VI, TIGER II

Looking formidable with its gun poised is this 1944 German PzKfw VI Tiger II tank preserved at Bovington.

      (K. A. Jenkinson)

The most powerful and heaviest tank to go into service in World War II, the PzKpfw VI Tiger II (Royal Tiger) entered production in December 1943. Built by Henschel, it was an improved version of the Tiger I with a longer barrelled, higher velocity 8.8 cm. gun and 2 × MG. It incorporated some of the most desirable features and components of the Panther II and was powered by a Maybach 700 hp. engine. It weighed 68.6 tons and was 23 ft. 10 in. long, 12 ft. 4 in. wide and 10 ft. 2 in. high, accommodating a crew of five. 485 were built before production ceased in March 1945.

Example Preserved.

      1944   Tank   Germ. Army RAC Museum, Bovington

PEERLESS

The Peerless armoured car was based on a Peerless lorry chassis of normal commercial use. The armoured bodywork was produced by the Austin Motor Company and the first one was completed in 1919. With an overall length of 14 ft. 6 in. and a weight of 5.8 tons, the Peerless was armed with 2 × Hotchkiss MG. Its power unit was a Peerless 40 hp. petrol engine and the vehicle was fitted with solid rubber tyres and twin rear wheels. It carried a crew of 4 and was unusual in having twin turrets. 100 were built, the last ones being completed in 1920.

Example Preserved.

1919   Armoured Car   Brit. Army   RAC Museum, Bovington

PERSHING M26

This American built M26 tank saw service with the U.S. Army before being saved for posterity.
(K. A. Jenkinson)

The American M26 heavy tank (later reclassified medium tank), given the name Pershing, was first built in 1945 although its design was started back in 1942. Powered by a Ford GAF V8 petrol engine, it was armed with 1 × 90 mm. gun and 1 × .3 in. co-axial MG, with 1 × .3 in. MG in its hull front and 1 × .5 in. MG on the turret roof. A number of variants were produced for special uses and the M26 was 28 ft. 5 in. long, 11 ft. 6 in. wide and 9 ft. 1 in. high. It remained in production until 1948.

Example Preserved.

1945   Tank   US Army   RAC Museum, Bovington

PHANOMEN GRANIT 25H

The Phanomen Granit 25H was a 4×2 normal control model introduced during the early 'thirties. Powered by a 4-cylinder petrol engine of 37 bhp., it had a 4-speed gearbox. Ambulance bodywork was fitted with accommodation for 4 stretchers or 8 sitting patients. The Granit 25H remained in production until 1939.

Example Preserved.

WPA155G 1935 Ambulance   Germ. Army Oliver, Eton Wick

PRAGA V3S

Of Czechoslovakian origin, the Praga V3S was a 3-ton 6×6 normal control model first introduced in 1953. Having a wheelbase of 4.14 m., it was fitted with a Praga T912-type 6-cylinder diesel engine of 7412 cc., built under licence from Tatra. It used a 4-speed gearbox with 2-speed transfer box and employed full air brakes. An optional 3½-ton winch could be fitted and the V3S remained in production until 1968. Numerous types of bodywork was fitted including cargo, tanker, workshop and van.

Example Preserved.

1953 G/S Cargo   Imperial War Museum, Duxford

PRAYING MANTIS

Built experimentally and never put into production was the Praying Mantis, one of which is now safe in preservation.

(K. A. Jenkinson)

Two experimental vehicles were built by County Commercial Cars Ltd. of Fleet, Hants. in 1943 and given the name Praying Mantis. This vehicle consisted of a slightly lengthened Universal Carrier chassis and was powered by a Ford V8 petrol engine. In place of the usual crew compartments was an armoured chamber in which the driver and gunner lay prone. This chamber was pivoted at the rear and could be elevated by means of a power take off from the main engine to a height of 11 ft. 6 in. above the ground. Armament was provided by 2×0.303 in. Bren LMG. The Praying Mantis was however never put into production and the project was cancelled in 1944.

Example Preserved.

	1943	Carrier	Brit. Army	RAC Museum, Bovington

RENAULT FT-17

The French built Renault FT-17 light tank was introduced in 1917. It was powered by a Renault 4-cylinder petrol engine of 35 bhp. and was armed with $1 \times$ Hotchkiss 8 mm. MG. In 1918 it was seen that Renault were unable to meet production demands and thus Berliet, Delaunay Belleville and SOMUA were given contracts and thus joined Renault in producing the FT-17. During 1918 the original armament was superceded by 1×37 mm. Puteaux gun and later in the year this was replaced with a 75 mm. gun. Large numbers of the FT-17 were built before production was ended in 1919.

Example Preserved.

66016	1917	Tank	French Army	RAC Museum, Bovington

RENAULT CHENILLETTE UE

88 371, a French Army Renault UE Chenillette supply carrier.

The Renault Chenillette UE supply carrier was introduced in 1931 for service with the French army. Having a crew of 2, it was very small with a length of 8 ft. 10 in., width of 5 ft. 7 in. and height of 3 ft. 5 in. It was fitted with a Renault 35 hp. 4 cylinder petrol engine and although generally unarmed, some were fitted with a Hotchkiss MG in a raised position on the right of the hull. Production ended in 1940 and a number of these UE's were later captured and used by the Germans.

Example Preserved.

88371	1939	Supply Carrier	French Army	RAC Museum, Bovington

REO M44

Introduced in 1950, the Reo 6×6 2½-ton M series were of normal control layout and were designed to replace the numerous 2½-ton World War II trucks still in service. Having a wheelbase of 12 ft. 10 in. the Reo M44 was powered by a Reo 6-cylinder petrol engine of 331 cu. in. and had a 5-speed gearbox with 2-speed transfer box. Its brakes were of the air-hydraulic type. Whilst the total M-series were available with a wide variety of bodywork, the M44 was supplied as a chassis/cab or as a bolster truck.

Example Preserved.

1952	Tractor	US Army	NWTM, Burtonwood

ROLLS ROYCE

Displayed at the RAF Museum at Bovington is this 1920 Rolls Royce armoured car.

Introduced in December 1914 using Rolls Royce Silver Ghost car chassis commandeered from the Rolls Royce factory shortly after the outbreak of World War I, this armoured car was powered by a Rolls Royce 6-cylinder 40-50 hp. engine. Armed with a .303 cal. Vickers MG mounted on a yoke in the turret and projecting through a hole in the armour plate, the chassis of this armoured car was fitted with twin rear wheels. In 1920 the original spoked wheels were replaced with those of the disc type, and the model continued in production until 1924.

Example Preserved.

1920   Armoured Car   Brit. Army   RAC Museum, Bovington

SALADIN

On display at Donington was this Saladin II, 06BB55.

(K. A. Jenkinson)

Although prototypes were built as early as 1952, the Saladin Armoured Car did not go into production until 1958. Being a 6×6 vehicle, it has three evenly spaced axles, the front two of which are fitted with power steering. Built by Alvis, the Saladin is powered by a Rolls Royce B80 straight eight petrol engine with pre-selector gearbox, its engine being rear mounted. Armament consists of 1×76 mm. medium velocity gun, 1×.3in. co-axial MG, 1×.3 in. MG (AA) and 12 smoke dischargers (6 either side at the front of the turret) whilst the vehicle is 16 ft. 2 in. long, 8 ft. 4 in. wide and 9 ft. 7 in. high. The Saladin remained in production until 1972.

Examples Preserved.

I		1958	Armoured Car	Brit. Army	RAC Museum, Bovington
II	06BB55	1962	Armoured Car	Brit. Army	Leyland Historic Vehicles Donington
II	00ED11		Armoured Car	Brit. Army	Imperial War Museum, Duxford

SCAMMELL EXPLORER

This Scammell Explorer was still in service when caught by the camera at a Military Vehicle Rally at Durham in 1980.

(K. A. Jenkinson)

The Scammell Explorer was introduced in 1950 as a recovery tractor for the Army, later being used additionally by the RAF as a heavy drawbar tractor with ballast box. Being a 10-ton 6×6 vehicle of normal control layout and having a wheelbase of 11 ft. 6 in., it was powered by a Meadows 6-cylinder engine of 181 bhp. and had a 6-speed gearbox. It was fitted with a 15-ton main winch and also had a 4½-ton power-operated jib winch. It remained in production in both military and civilian forms until the 'sixties.

Example Preserved.

DBD294T	1952	Recovery Tractor	Brit. Army	Walker, Market Harborough

SCAMMELL MH6

The Scammell MH6, better known as the mechanical horse is a 3×2 tractor unit designed for coupling to a semi-trailer and having a carrying capacity of 6-tons. First introduced in 1933 it has a wheelbase of 9 ft. 2¾ in. and is powered by a 4-cylinder 1125 cc. Scammell petrol engine, having a 4-speed gearbox and double reduction rear axle. 676 were built for use by the Royal Navy during World War II, the MH6 being built for civilian use until 1948.

Examples Preserved.

73YY89	1944	Tractor	Royal Navy	Giles, Bewdley
75YY30	1944	Tractor	Royal Navy	Norgate, Leamington

SCAMMELL PIONEER R100

Affectionately know as the 'Coffee Pot Scammell', the Pioneer R100 has seen valued service in both military and civilian roles. This example is now safely preserved at Duxford.

(D. Game)

Based upon Scammell's tractor unit first introduced in 1927, the Pioneer R100 went into production in 1939. Designed as a heavy artillery tractor it was a 6 × 4 normal control unit powered by a Gardner 6LW oil engine. Transmission was via a 6-speed gearbox and had air brakes. Its wheelbase was 12 ft. 2 in. and its overall weight 8 tons 9½ cwt. The Pioneer R100 remained in production until 1945.

Examples Preserved.

FBV371	1937	Transporter	Brit. Army	Simmonds, Tonbridge
HVW77	1939	Artillery Tractor	Brit. Army	Perrett, Saffron Walden
KBW575L	1939	Artillery Tractor	Brit. Army	Barber, Hayling Island
MOW389	1939		Brit. Army	Private Owner
RBP166M	1939	Artillery Tractor	Brit. Army	Adams, Petersfield
RMG623	1939		Brit. Army	Private Owner
806FUF	1939	Wrecker	Brit. Army	Willis, New Haw
	1939	Wrecker	Brit. Army	Franklin, Ashwell
	1939	Artillery Tractor	Brit. Army	Oakfield, Princes Risborough
	1939	Artillery Tractor	Brit. Army	Andrews, Hertford Heath
48RB50	1939		Brit. Army	SEME, Bordon
	1940	Artillery Tractor	Brit. Army	Parker, Sussex
M191088	1941	Artillery Tractor	Brit. Army	Barber, Bournemouth
	1941	Wrecker		Blackmore, Ashwell
	1942	Wrecker	Brit. Army	Mortimer, Salisbury
FUF47	1942	Wrecker	Brit. Army	Warnham War Museum
	1942	Wrecker	Brit. Army	Harverson, Rusper

FFD520T	1942			Roberts, Enville
	1942	Artillery Tractor	Brit. Army	Peters, Sussex
	1942	Wrecker	Brit. Army	Harvey, Salisbury
NO4810	1943	Artillery Tractor	Brit. Army	Walmsley & Lovegrove, Duxford
121YKO	1943	Artillery Tractor	Brit. Army	Bramley, Gravesend
	1943	Artillery Tractor	Brit. Army	Rex, High Cross
50CWT	1944	Wrecker	RAF	Whitaker, Sowerby Bridge

SCORPION

Preserved from a more recent era is this Scorpion tracked reconnaissance vehicle dating from 1970.
(K. A. Jenkinson)

The Scorpion was a tracked reconnaissance vehicle built for the army by Alvis. The first prototype was completed in 1969, with full production starting late in 1971. It has 5 road wheels on each side and is the first vehicle of all aluminium construction to be accepted into service with the British Army. Powered by a Jaguar 6-cylinder petrol engine, it carries a crew of 3 and is armed with 1×76 mm. gun and 1×7.62 co-axial MG and has 3 smoke dischargers on each side of its turret. It is 14 ft. 5 in. long, 7 ft. 2 in. wide and 6 ft. 10 in. high. The Scorpion is still being produced.

Example Preserved.

OOSP97	1970	Reconnaissance	Brit. Army	RAC Museum, Bovington

SENTINEL

Used for towing aircraft was the Sentinel Douglas tractor.

(D. Game)

Introduced in 1961, the Sentinel was an improved version of the Douglas Tugmaster. Of 4×4 configuration with normal control layout, it had a wheelbase of 9 ft. 2 in. and was powered by a Rolls Royce B80-type 8-cylinder engine of 160 bhp. It had a 4-speed semi-automatic gearbox with 2-speed transfer box and was equipped with air brakes and power assisted steering. A generating set was incorporated into its bodywork, as was a 6-7-ton winch and the Sentinel was used by the RAF as an aircraft towing tractor. It remained in production until around 1970.

Examples Preserved.

| 1963 | Heavy towing tractor | RAF | Duxford Aviation Society, Duxford |
| 1964 | Heavy towing tractor | RAF | Imperial War Museum, Duxford |

SENTINEL AC1

Built in Australia for the Australian Army was the Sentinel AC1 tank, an example of which has been preserved.

(K. A. Jenkinson)

Officially designated Cruiser Tank AC1, the Sentinel was Australian built. The prototype made its appearance in January 1942 and after undergoing trials it was put into full production in August of that year. It had a cast one-piece hull with prominent armoured sleeve for bow machine gun mounting and was built at the Chullona Tank Assembly Shops, New South Wales (this having been started in January 1942 by New South Wales State Railways). Power for the Sentinel was provided by 3 Cadillac V8 117 hp. petrol engines arranged in 'clover leaf' formation and the complete vehicle was 20 ft. 9 in. long, 9 ft. 1 in. wide and 8 ft. 5 in. high. It was armed with 1 × 2 pdr. OQF and 2 × Vickers .303 cal. MG.

Example Preserved.

1942	Tank	Australian. Army	RAC Museum, Bovington

SEXTON

The Sexton was a self-propelled gun, the pilot model of which was completed in 1942. Built in Canada at the Montreal Locomotive Works Tank Arsenal, the Sexton was widely used by both the British and Canadian Forces. Its chassis was based on that of the Canadian medium tank, the Ram II, its Continental engine and transmission being almost identical to the Ram II. Armament was provided by 1 × 25 pdr. C Mk.II gun and 2 × unmounted Brownings. The Sexton carried a crew of 6 and had a length of 19 ft. 3 in. Some 2,150 had been built when production ceased towards the end of 1945.

Example Preserved.

762541	1943	S.P. Gun	Brit. Army	Imperial War Museum, Duxford

SHERMAN

One of the best known tanks of World War II was the Sherman, built in the U.S.A. for use by the British Army. Several have survived including this Sherman II.

(K. A. Jenkinson)

Designated Medium Tank M4 in its homeland, the USA, this tank was given the name Sherman when delivered to the British Army. The M4 pilot was built by Lima Locomotive Works in February 1941 and when production started later in that year, several firms were contracted including Pacific Car & Foundry Co., Fisher, Ford and Pressed Steel. The first Shermans supplied to the British army were shipped to the 8th Army in the Middle East in October 1942 and during the next three years, the Sherman was more widely used in British service than any other tank. Numerous variants were built both as basic models and for special purposes. Amongst these were the Sherman II which was based on the American M4A1. This was similar to the original M4 but had a cast hull and was mounted with 1×75 mm. M3 gun, $2 \times .30$ cal. MG and $1 \times .50$ cal. MG (AA). It was powered by a Continental R-975 engine of 340 hp. and was 19 ft. 4 in. long, 8 ft. 7 in. wide and 9 ft. 0 in. high. The Sherman VC Firefly was the British designation for the M4A4, this being fitted with the Chrysler WC Multibank engine, made from five commercial automobile engines on a common drive shaft. This provided 370 hp. and to accommodate it, the rear hull had to be lengthened giving the vehicle an overall length of 19 ft. 10½ in. The major development of the VC Firefly however was the fitting of a 17 pdr. gun, making it the most powerfully armed British tank of the war. To increase ammunition stowage, the hull machine gun (and gunner) was deleted.

Of the special purpose variants, the Sherman III DD was given Straussler duplex drive equipment. This proved a most successful method of giving amphibious capability to a standard tank. Introduced in April 1943, the Sherman III DD was waterproofed and fitted with a collapsable canvas screen round the hull top, struts locking this into place. Two small propellers driven from the power take-off of the vehicle's engine provided propulsion at 4 knots through the water, these being declutched and folded away when on land. The power unit for the Sherman III DD were twin General Motors 6-71 diesel engines.

The Sherman Crab was developed in June 1943 for mine clearing purposes. Its rotor had 43 flailing chains which beat the ground ahead of the vehicle and below the rotor arms were wire cutters for clearing barbed wire.

Examples Preserved.

I	1943	Tank	Brit. Army	RAC Museum, Bovington
II	1942	Tank	Brit. Army	RAC Museum, Bovington
III	1943	Tank	Brit. Army	RAC Museum, Bovington
CRAB	1944	Tank	Brit. Army	RAC Museum, Bovington
VC T228796	1944	Tank	Brit. Army	RAC Museum, Bovington
			Brit. Army	Imperial War Museum, Duxford
			Brit. Army	Imperial War Museum, London

SONDERKRAFTFAHRZEUG 234/3

The SdKfz 234/3 was an 8-wheeled heavy armoured car which first appeared in 1944. Designed by the Czechoslovakian firm of Tatra, it had a single long mudguard on each side containing four stowage lockers. Designed as a basic reconnaissance vehicle, it was powered by an air cooled Tatra V12 diesel engine of 220 hp. and could accommodate a crew of 4. Armed with 1×7.5 cm. assault gun and $1 \times MG$, it was 19 ft. 9 in. long, 7 ft. 9 in. wide and 7 ft. 6 in. high.

Example Preserved.

1944	Armoured Car	Germ. Army	RAC Museum, Bovington

SONDERKRAFTFAHRZEUG 251.

Introduced into service in 1940, the SdKfz 251 was a half-tracked armoured vehicle built in Germany by Hanomag. Over twenty different versions were built for a multitude of uses, but all used the same basic mechanical specification. Powered by a Maybach 120 hp. engine and having a length of 19 ft. 0 in., width of 6 ft. 11 in. and height of 5 ft. 9 in., the 251 weighed over 8 tons. It was armed with $1 \times MG$ and could carry a crew of 12. The SdKfz remained in production until 1944.

Example Preserved.

1942	ATV	Germ. Army	RAC Museum, Bovington

SPA TL37

The SPA TL37 was introduced in 1936, being a normal control 4×4 light artillery tractor with a wheelbase of 2.5 m. Built in Italy it was powered by a Spa 4-cylinder petrol engine of 4053 cc., and had a 5-speed gearbox and mechanically operated brakes. It was available with pneumatic or solid tyres and had 4-wheel steering. It could also be fitted with truck bodywork and remained in production until 1948.

Example Preserved.

Artillery Tractor   Italian Army Ottewill, Somerset

SPAHPANZER LUCHS

The German built Spahpanzer was an 8×8 reconnaissance vehicle. The first two prototypes were built by Daimler Benz in 1975, full production starting the following year built by Rheinstahl. Powered by a Daimler Benz 10-cylinder multi-fuel engine of 390 bhp., the vehicle was fully amphibious, being propelled in the water by 2 propellers at the rear of the hull. A full range of night vision equipment was fitted and it was armed with 1×20 mm. cannon, 1×7.62 mm. MG (AA) and 2×4 smoke dischargers each side of the turret. The Spahpanzer had full 8×8 drive and could also be driven backwards at maximum speed. 500 had been built when production ended in 1977.

Example Preserved.

1977 Reconnaissance   Germ. Army RAC Museum, Bovington

STAGHOUND

The Staghound, American built for the British Army was a 4 × 4 armoured car, this example dating from 1942.

(K. A. Jenkinson)

Built in the USA by Chevrolet, the T17E1 was built for the British army who gave it the name Staghound. Built as a 4 × 4 armoured car, it was powered by 2 Chevrolet 6-cylinder engines and had hydramatic transmission. Its most serious design defect was the lack of provision for driving in reverse. Introduced in 1942, the Mk.I was armed with 1 × 37 mm. gun and 1 × .30 in. co-axial MG with 1 × .30 in. Browning MG in the hull front. On the Mk.II introduced in 1943, a 3 in. Howitzer was used whilst the Mk.III which made its debut later in 1943 was armed with 1 × 75 mm. gun and 1 × 7.92 mm. co-axial Besa MG. The Staghound remained in production until 1943.

Example Preserved.

1942　Armoured Car　　Brit. Army　　RAC Museum, Bovington

Preserved in RAF colours is KPU237, a Standard 12 utility with original style radiator grille.

(C. Pearce)

First produced at the end of 1939, the Standard 12 is a 4 × 2 light utility based on the Standard Flying Twelve civilian car chassis. At first it retained the civilian type radiator grille, this being changed early in 1940 to one of flat wire mesh. Having a wheelbase of 9 ft. 0 in. it was designed as a 5-cwt. utility and has as its power unit, a Standard 12 hp. 4-cylinder petrol engine with a bore and stroke of 69.5 mm. × 106 mm. Transmission is via a 4-speed gearbox and single dry plate clutch to a semi-floating, spiral bevel rear axle whilst the brakes are mechanically operated acting on all wheels. Its body has fixed sides and drop tailboard, and a detachable canvas tilt is carried on three hoops. The Standard 12 remained in production until 1944.

Examples Preserved.

NPN156	1939	Utility		Groombridge, Heathfield
KKP210	1940	Utility	Brit. Army	Smith, Horbury
	1941	Utility		Butcher, Middx.
	1942	Utility		Worthing, Salop
KPU237	1942	Utility	RAF	Sarjantson, Sawbridge-worth
NRP650	1942	Utility		Private Owner
	1942	Van	RAF	Dransfield, Horbury

STANDARD BEAVERETTE

Looking quite formidable is this World War II Standard Beaverette armoured car.

(P. Issaac)

Making its appearance in 1940, the Standard Beaverette was a light reconnaissance armoured vehicle based on the Standard 14 hp. civilian car chassis. Having a wheelbase of 9 ft. 0 in., it was of normal control layout and was powered by a Standard 4-cylinder 14 hp. petrol engine, transmission being via a 4-speed gearbox. Armament was provided by 1×0.303 in. Bren light machine gun and $1 \times$ Boys anti-tank rifle. A crew of 3 was carried. The Mk IV had a shortened wheelbase of 6 ft. 2 in.

Examples Preserved.

1940	Reconnaissance	Brit. Army	Pearce, Holywell
1941	Reconnaissance	Brit. Army	Groombridge, Heathfield
1942	Reconnaissance	Brit. Army	Isaac, Umberleigh
1942	Reconnaissance	Brit. Army	Bygraves, Baldock
1943	Reconnaissance	Brit. Army	Mutch, Aberlady

STEYR 1500A

The German Army used the Steyr 1500A both as command cars and as personnel carriers.

(K. A. Jenkinson)

The Steyr 1500A, first introduced in 1941 was a 4×4 normal control vehicle with a wheelbase of 10 ft. 6¼ in. Powered by a V8 petrol engine of 85 bhp., it had a 4-speed gearbox with 2-speed transfer box. The chassis of the 1500A was produced by Steyr in Austria and Auto-Union and it could be fitted with either 8-seater personnel or command car bodywork. The 1500A remained in production until 1944.

Examples Preserved.

	1942	Command Car	Germ. Army	National Motor Museum, Beaulieu.
	1943	Personnel Carrier	Germ. Army	Kenton, London
NOY597E	1944	Personnel Carrier	Germ. Army	Oliver, Eton Wick

STRIDSVAGN m/40

Swedish built, this Stridsvagn m/40 dates from 1940.

(K. A. Jenkinson)

The Swedish built Stridsvagn m/40 light tank entered production in 1940 for use by the Swedish army. Originally designated m/40L, it was fitted with a Scania-Vabis 6-cylinder 142 hp. petrol engine and was 16 ft. 1 in. long, 6 ft. 11 in. wide and 6 ft. 10 in. high. It was armed with 1 × 37 mm. gun and 2 × 8 mm. co-axial MG's. In 1941 the m/40L was superseded by the m/40K, this being an improved model with heavier armour and powered by a Scania-Vabis 6-cylinder 160 hp. petrol engine. Like the m/40L, it carried a crew of 3 and retained the same armament. The m/40K was discontinued in 1944.

Example Preserved.

1940	Tank	Swedish Army	RAC Museum, Bovington

STUART M5

Serving mainly as a light tank during the Second World War was the Stuart M5, a type of which several examples have been preserved.

(K. A. Jenkinson)

Introduced in the early part of 1942, the Light Tank M5 was originally built by the Cadillac Division of GMC in the USA. Its design owed much to the M3 from which it was adapted and it was easily distinguishable from the M3 by its rear engine covers which were stepped up in order to accommodate its twin Cadillac V8 engines of 220 hp. In September 1942 the M5 underwent a number of design improvements and was re-designated M5A1. To speed up production, Massey-Harris also began building the M5A1 during the summer of 1943 under the 'parentage' of Cadillac. Of 15 ft. 10½ in. length, 7 ft. 4½ in. width and 7 ft. 6½ in. height, the M5A1 was mounted with 1 × 37 mm. gun M6 and 2 × .30 cal. Browning MG. Most M3A1s additionally had AA MG. As well as serving in a Light Tank role, a number of other variants of the M5A1 were built for specific AFV duties.

Examples Preserved.

M5	1942	Tank	Brit. Army	Warnham War Museum
M5A1	1943		Brit. Army	RAC Museum, Bovington
	1944		Brit. Army	Imperial War Museum, Duxford
	1944		Brit. Army	Marchant, Milton Keynes
	1944		Brit. Army	Groombridge, Heathfield
	1944		Brit. Army	Ross, Kent
	1944		Brit. Army	Arnold, Kent

STUDEBAKER WEASEL M29

Built as a fully tracked cargo carrier, the Studebaker Weasel M29 enjoyed a long production run.
(K. A. Jenkinson)

The Studebaker Weasel M29 was a fully tracked cargo carrier which made its debut in 1942. Powered by a Studebaker 'Champion' 6-cylinder petrol engine it had a 3-speed gearbox with 2-speed transfer box and whilst early production models had 15 in. tracks, later M29 Weasels had 20 in. tracks. It was 10 ft. 6 in. long, 5 ft. 6 in. wide and 5 ft. 11 in. high. It remained in production until 1945.

Examples Preserved.

4037585	1943	Carrier	US Army	Warnham War Museum
40151811	1944	Carrier		Arthurs & Halls, Durham
	1944	Carrier	Norwegian Army	
				Anderson, Otterburn

STUDEBAKER WEASEL M29C

Differing from the Studebaker Weasel M29, the M29C was an amphibious cargo carrier.

(K. A. Jenkinson)

The Studebaker Weasel M29C was an amphibious cargo carrier first put into production in 1943. Water propulsion was effected by its tracks and it was powered by a Studebaker 6-cylinder 65 bhp. petrol engine. Transmission was via a 3-speed gearbox with 2-speed final drive at rear. The Weasel M29C was 16 ft. 0 in. long, 5 ft. 7¼ in. wide and 5 ft. 11 in. high. It remained in production in the USA until 1945.

Examples Preserved.

	1943	Amphibian	US Army	Warnham War Museum
OKX866M	1943	Amphibian		Beddall, Iver
	1943	Amphibian	US Army	Simmers, Aberdeen
	1944	Amphibian	US Army	Chapman, Kettering
	1944	Amphibian		Pagano, Saffron Walden
	1944	Amphibian		Bowman, Blaydon
	1944	Amphibian		RAC Museum, Bovington
	1944	Amphibian		Davie & Hall, Durham
	1944	Amphibian		Taylor, Consett

STUDEBAKER US6×4

Built extensively for Lend-Lease, the Studebaker US6×4 was introduced in 1941. Of normal control layout, it was a 2½ ton 6×4 truck with a wheelbase of 13 ft. 6 in. and was powered by a Hercules JXD-type 6-cylinder petrol engine of 87 bhp. and had a 5-speed gearbox. Later in 1941 a 2-speed transfer box was also fitted. Cargo bodywork was fitted with open or closed cab and some were given a winch. A tractor version was also produced, this having a wheelbase of 12 ft. 4 in. The Studebaker US6×4 remained in production until 1945.

Examples Preserved.

	1942	G/S Truck	US Army	Chapman, Kettering
GAB919	1943	G/S Truck	US Army	Groombridge, Heathfield
	1943	G/S Truck	US Army	Page, Norwich

STURMGESCHUTZ III

The German built Sturmgeschutz III was an armoured self-propelled gun to support infantry. The chassis used was that of the Panzerkampfwagen III, the turret being replaced by a low fixed superstructure running up to the drivers plate. Armed with 1×7.5 cm. gun, it was powered by a Maybach V12 petrol engine of 300 bhp. The Sturmgeschutz III was first placed in service in 1940 and remained in production throughout World War II—with various modifications. By the time production ceased in 1945, over 10,500 had been built.

Example Preserved.

1943   S.P. Gun   Germ. Army RAC Museum, Bovington

SU-76

The Russian SU-76 light self-propelled gun is seen here after being acquired for preservation by the RAC Museum at Bovington.

(K. A. Jenkinson)

Entering production early in 1942, the Russian-built SU-76 was a light self-propelled gun. Armed with 1×76.2 mm. gun, it was 16 ft. 5 in. long, 8 ft. 11 in. wide and 7 ft. 3 in. high. The first series of SU-76 were powered by two GAZ-202 6-cylinder petrol engines mounted one on each side of the vehicle but after these, the engines were mounted in tandem. In 1943 an improved version was introduced designated SU-76M, but following the discontinuing of the original SU-76, the SU-76M lost its suffix and was then known plainly as the SU-76. Over 12,600 were built before production ended in 1945.

Example Preserved.

1943   S.P. Gun   Russian Army RAC Museum, Bovington

SU-100

Also of Russian origin is the SU-100 medium self-propelled gun of which this example was built in 1945.

(K. A. Jenkinson)

The Soviet-built SU-100 medium self-propelled gun first entered production in September 1944 at Uralmashzavod. Its design was such that the driver was separated from the other 3 crew members by armour plate, and as a result an internal communications system was necessary. Fitted with a 12-cylinder diesel engine, the SU-100 was 31 ft. 0 in. long, 9 ft. 10 in. wide and 7 ft. 4 in. high. It was armed with 1 × 100 mm. gun and 2 × 7.62 mm. SMG, and it remained in production until 1957.

Examples Preserved.

1945	S.P. Gun	Russian Army	RAC Museum, Bovington
1948		Russian Army	Imperial War Museum, Duxford

Although the T14 heavy assault tank never entered production, one of the prototypes has been saved for posterity.

(K. A. Jenkinson)

The T14 was a heavy assault tank designed in the USA to meet British requirements. An agreement for 8,500 of these Ford tanks was concluded with the Ordnance Department in 1943 and two pilot models were completed in 1943. Trials showed that modifications were needed to the track and suspension and after this was carried out, one of the pilot models was sent to Britain in 1944. By this time, British tank requirements had changed, however, and in view of Britain's loss of interest, the Ordnance Department dropped the project in December 1944 without the T14 having entered production. Built to carry a crew of 5, the T14 was 20 ft. 4 in. long, 10 ft. 3 in. wide and 9 ft. 1 in. high. It was powered by a Ford GAZ V8 petrol engine of 520 hp. and carried 1 × 75 mm. M3 gun, 2 × .30 cal. Browning MG and 1 × .50 cal. Browning MG (AA).

Example Preserved.

| 1942 | Tank | Brit. Army | RAC Museum, Bovington |

This rear view of one of the preserved T34 heavy tanks shows its clean lines and large size.

(K. A. Jenkinson)

The American Heavy Tank T34 resulted from the adaptation of the standard American 120 mm. AA gun to a form suitable for mounting in a tank. One each T29 and T30 tanks were modified and fitted with this gun and were then redesignated T34, the pilot models of which were not delivered until 1947. No production models followed, but the T34 was used in the design of the later M103.

Examples Preserved.

1944	Tank	Russian Army	Imperial War Museum, Duxford
1944		Russian Army	RAC Museum, Bovington

The T54 was one of the main Soviet battle tanks of the 'fifties.

(K. A. Jenkinson)

The Soviet T54 main battle tank was built in Russia, Czechoslovakia, Poland and China, the first prototype appearing in 1947. Full production did not commence, however, until 1950. Powered by an air-cooled 12-cylinder diesel engine the T54 is 21 ft. 2 in. long, 10 ft. 9 in. wide and 7 ft. 10 in. high. It is armed with 1 × 100 mm. gun and 1 × 7.62 mm. co-axial MG, 1 × 7.62 mm. MG in the bow and 1 × 12.7 mm. MG (AA), and was fitted with a full range of infra-red night driving equipment. The T54 remained in production until 1960 by which time over 45,000 had been built.

Example Preserved.

1954	Tank	Russian Army	RAC Museum, Bovington

TANK MARK I

Entering production in 1916, the Mark I was the first tracked armoured fighting vehicle to be built in quantity, with a total of 150 being produced. Constructed by two manufacturers—Fosters and Metropolitan Carriage, Wagon & Finance Co., both male and female versions were built. The male was armed with 2 × 6 pdr. and 4 × Hotchkiss MG whilst the female had 4 × Vickers MG and 1 × Hotchkiss MG. The engine used was a Daimler 105 hp. unit and the male was 32 ft. 6 in. long, 13 ft. 9 in. wide and 8 ft. 0½ in. high.

Example Preserved.

1916	Tank	Brit. Army	RAC Museum, Bovington

TANK MARK II

Introduced in 1916, the Mark II was really an improved version of the Mark I, the chief difference being that the Mark II did not have the tail wheel. A new type of cast iron track roller was used and a wider track plate fitted at every sixth position on the track. Only fifty were built before the introduction of the Mark III. The male was armed with 2×6 pdr. and $4 \times$ Hotchkiss MG whilst the female was given $6 \times$ Hotchkiss MG. Both used a Daimler 105 hp. engine, and had a length of 26 ft. 5 in., width of 13 ft. 9 in. (female 14 ft. 4 in.) and height of 8 ft. 0½ in.

Examples Preserved.

	1916	Tank	Brit. Army	RAC Museum, Bovington

TANK MARK IV

This British Mark IV Female tank dates from 1917.

(K. A. Jenkinson)

Although externally similar to the Mark I, the Mark IV incorporated numerous detail improvements gained from the operation of the earlier marks. Crew conditions were improved with new ventilation systems and better means of escape whilst the engine was given a vacuum petrol feed system in place of the earlier gravity feed type. 420 males and 595 females were built, the first of which was placed in service in 1917. The male carried armament of 2×6 pdr. guns and $4 \times$ Lewis MG whereas the female had $6 \times$ Lewis MG. A 105 hp. Daimler engine was used and the Mark IV was 26 ft. 5 in. long, 13 ft. 6 in. wide (10 ft. 6 in. wide female) and 8 ft. 1 in. high. It carried a crew of 8.

Examples Preserved.

Female	1917	Tank	Brit. Army	RAC Museum, Bovington
Male	1917		Brit. Army	RAC Museum, Bovington

TANK MARK V

Entering production in 1918, the Mark V was the first heavy tank that could be controlled by one man. Although developed from the Mark I, it incorporated many design changes and was fitted with a Ricardo 150 hp. engine. 200 males and 200 females were built during 1918, each of which carried a crew of 8. The external dimensions were 26 ft. 5 in. long, 13 ft. 6 in. wide (female 10 ft. 6 in.) and 8 ft. 8 in. high. The male was equipped with 2×6 pdr. guns and 4×Hotchkiss MG whilst the female had 6×Hotchkiss MG.

Examples Preserved.

	1918	Tank	Brit. Army	RAC Museum, Bovington
ME9828			Brit. Army	Imperial War Museum, London

TANK MARK V**

The Mark V** was merely a lengthened version of the Mark V, with a larger capacity engine and greater armament. Designed for a crew of 8, it was given a Ricardo 225 hp. engine and was built in both male and female versions. Its length was 32 ft. 5 in. and width 13 ft. 6 in. (female 10 ft. 6 in.) with a height of 9 ft. 0 in. The male carried 2×6 pdr. guns and 5×Hotchkiss MG whilst the female was mounted with 7×Hotchkiss MG. The Mark V** was built during 1918.

Example Preserved.

Female	1918	Tank	Brit. Army	RAC Museum, Bovington

TANK MARK VIII

Put into production towards the end of World War I was the British Mark VIII tank, a Male example of which is shown here.

(K. A. Jenkinson)

Following the entry of the USA into the war in 1917, an agreement was reached for a joint Allied tank to be produced in a new factory in France with the United Kingdom supplying the armament and most of the materials for the hull and the USA supplying the engine and other mechanical parts. Being based upon earlier British designs, the Mark VIII first appeared in July 1918, fitted with a Liberty 300 hp. aero engine. After the hostilities ceased, the large order for these Allied tanks was cancelled but 100 were completed in America and 7 in England. The first British tank had a Rolls-Royce engine, but this was later given two 6-cylinder 150 hp. Ricardo engines geared together as one unit, as were all the others. Armed with 2×6 pdr. guns and $7 \times$ Hotchkiss MG, the Mark VIII was 34 ft. 2½ in. long, 12 ft. 4 in. wide and 10 ft. 3 in. high.

Example Preserved.

Male	1919	Tank	Brit. Army	RAC Museum, Bovington

TANK MARK IX

Dating from 1918 is this Mark IX British tank.

(K. A. Jenkinson)

Introduced in October 1918, the Mark IX was specially designed as an infantry or supplies carrier. Its Ricardo 150 hp. engine was placed well forward, just behind the driver's cab leaving a long, clear compartment with access via two large oval doors. In addition to its crew to its crew of 4, 10 tons of stores or 50 infantrymen could be carried. The Mark IX was 31 ft. 10 in. long, 8 ft. 1 in. wide and 8 ft. 5 in. high and was armed with 2 × Hotchkiss MG. Only 35 Mark IXs were ever built.

Example Preserved.

1918   Tank   Brit. Army   RAC Museum, Bovington

TETRARCH

This Tetrarch light tank dating from 1940 was one of many built during World War II.

(K. A. Jenkinson)

First built in 1938, this light tank Mk.VII was known unofficially as the 'Purdah'. Designed by Vickers, the Mk.VII adopted a novel type of suspension incorporating large road wheels but, as with some earlier Vickers designs, steering was achieved by flexing the tracks. When the war seemed inevitable, Vickers were asked to transfer production to Metropolitan Cammell to be free to do other work. Although 240 were ordered, only 177 were actually built, the first one coming off the production line in November 1940. The development of airborne forces suggested the adoption of the Light Mk.VII for the glider-borne role. In 1943 the name Tetrarch was adopted and the Hamlicar glider was specially designed to carry one of these light tanks. Their first action was on 6th June 1944 and a few Tetrarchs remained in use until 1949. Of 13 ft. 6 in. length, the Tetrarch was 7 ft. 7 in. wide and 6ft. 11½ in. high and was mounted with a 1 × 2 pdr. QFSA and 1 × 7.92 mm. Besa MG. All the Tetrarchs built were fitted with Meadows 12-cylinder, 165 hp. engines.

Example Preserved.

1940	Tank	Brit. Army	RAC Museum, Bovington

THORNYCROFT AMAZON WF.

The Thornycroft Amazon WF was introduced in 1940, being a 6-ton 6 × 4 model of normal control layout. Two variants were built, one with a wheelbase of 11 ft. 9 in., the other with 16 ft. 6 in. The short wheelbase model was fitted with a Thornycroft 6-cylinder petrol engine of 100 bhp., whilst the LWB version had a Thornycroft 6-cylinder diesel engine of 105 bhp. Both shared the same transmission, this being a 4-speed gearbox with 2-speed transfer box. A number of the LWB Amazons were fitted with petrol engines. The Amazon was fitted with a Coles turntable crane which had a maximum capacity of 5 tons and 1,432 SWB and 388 LWB vehicles were built, the majority for service with the RAF before production ended in 1945.

Examples Preserved.

	1943	Crane		Lovegrove, Bromley
174ONK	1943	Crane		Dixon, Much Hadham
18TNK	1945	Crane	RAF	Dixon, Much Hadham

THORNYCROFT 'BIG BEN'

Introduced in 1953, the Thornycroft Big Ben SM/GRN6 was a 10-ton 6 × 4 vehicle of forward control layout. Available as a truck with 16 ft. 9 in. wheelbase or as a tractor with 13 ft. 6 in. wheelbase, it was powered by a 6-cylinder engine developing 180 bhp. and had a 4-speed gearbox with 2-speed transfer box and two-line air pressure brakes. Marshall bodywork was fitted to the canvas tilt truck whilst the tractor was used to pull a semi-trailer with house type body or as a missile transporter. The Big Ben was also available to the civilian market.

Example Preserved.

	Office	Brit. Army	NWTM, Burtonwood

THORNYCROFT NUBIAN

Seen here in 'as acquired' condition, this Thornycroft Nubian requires many hours of hard work to return it to its original glory.

(P. Isaac)

The Thornycroft Nubian was introduced in June 1940 as a 4×4 3-ton model with forward control layout. Powered by a Thornycroft AC4-type 4-cylinder petrol engine, it had a 4-speed gearbox with 2-speed transfer box and epicyclic hub reduction gears. Its wheelbase was 12 ft. 0 in. and it was available with a variety of bodywork types. It remained in production after the end of World War II for civilian use and was then available with either an AEC oil engine or its Thornycroft unit.

Example Preserved.

| 1941 | G/S Truck | RAF. | Hoare, Chepstow |

THORNYCROFT ZS/TC4

Introduced in 1940, the Thornycroft ZS/TC4 was a 3 ton 4×2 normal control vehicle with a wheelbase of 13 ft. 4 in. It was fitted with a Thornycroft 4-cylinder 3900 cc. petrol engine and had a 4-speed gearbox and hydraulic brakes. Used mainly as a searchlight vehicle, it remained in production until 1945 by which time 1,576 had been built.

Example Preserved.

| BWW344H 1941 | Searchlight | Searle, Marsham |

TOG II

This TOG IIA of 1942 vintage served with the British Army during World War II.

(K. A. Jenkinson)

The TOG II heavy tank was developed from the TOG I which had first appeared as a prototype in October 1940. Designed and built by Foster's of Lincoln, the TOG was built to an outmoded concept but nevertheless incorporated ingenious but complicated mechanical features. Although the TOG II was used for trials, the Churchill A22 had by that time appeared and had been accepted as the standard heavy infantry tank and thus the TOG II had been superseded before it had ever reached the production stage. However, in 1942 it was fitted with a new turret and 17 pdr. gun and used for further tests before being dropped completely. Powered by a Paxman-Richardo V12 600 hp. diesel engine with electric transmission, the TOG II was armed with 1 × 17 pdr. QF with no secondary armament being fitted. Its overall dimensions were 33 ft. 3 in. length, 10 ft. 3 in. width and 10 ft. 0 in. height.

Example Preserved.

IIA   1942   Tank   Brit. Army   RAC Museum, Bovington

TORTOISE

This heavily armoured assault tank, the Tortoise, bearing number JLR98 is now preserved as a reminder of the latter World War II era.

(K. A. Jenkinson)

Designated Heavy Assault Tank A39, the Tortoise was a very heavily armoured vehicle mounted with a super-heavy gun. Although the first Tortoise, built by Nuffield Mechanisations & Aero was scheduled for completion, in August 1945, it was in fact the following year before this pilot model was delivered for trials. It was quickly followed by a further five pilots, but due to the war having by this time ended, no more were built and the design was dropped. Built for a crew of seven, the Tortoise was powered by a Rolls Royce Meteor V12 600 hp. engine and was armed with 1 × 32 pdr. OQF and 3 × 7.92 Besa MG. It was 33 ft. 0 in. long, 12 ft. 10 in. wide and 10 ft. 0 in. high.

Example Preserved.

JLR98   1945   Tank   Brit. Army   RAC Museum, Bovington

TROJAN

The Trojan was widely used by the RAF as a tender vehicle prior to and during the early part of the second great war.

The Trojan was widely used by the RAF as a tender. Introduced in 1926 it was a 4 × 2 model of normal control layout with a wheelbase of 8 ft. 0 in. It was fitted with a Trojan 4-cylinder, 2-stroke petrol engine rated at 10 hp. whilst transmission was via a 2-speed epicyclic gearbox to a chain drive rear axle. The handbrake operated on the transmission whilst the foot brake acted on the rear wheels. This particular model remained in production until 1933.

Example Preserved.

VB8081	1930	Tender	RAF	Simes, Reigate

VALENTINE

Built in various forms, this is the Archer variant of the famous Valentine tank.

(K. A. Jenkinson)

Built by Vickers, the Infantry Tank Mk.III Valentine first went into production in 1940 without a pilot model having been built. Based upon the A10 design, updated and improved, the Valentine played an important role in the desert battles, being used in a cruiser tank role with armoured divisions of the army. Metropolitan Cammell and Birmingham Railway Carriage & Wagon Works joined Vickers in the production of the Valentine—of which no fewer than 23 variants were built and 8,275 were constructed before production was discontinued in the early part of 1944. In addition to these, 1,420 were built in Canada by Canadian Pacific and all but 30 of these which were retained for training purposes were delivered to the Soviet Army. The Valentine III was given a modified turret to accommodate a third crew member whilst the Valentine Bridgelayer was a Valentine II with turret removed and adapted to carry No. 1 30 ft. scissors bridge. Hydraulic rams and arms were fitted for launch and recovery and hydraulic equipment fitted into the turret space. The Valentine was of 17 ft. 9 in. length, 8 ft. 7½ in. width and 7 ft. 5½ in. height and was powered by an AEC 131 hp. diesel engine. Its armament consisted of 1 × 2 pdr. gun and co-axial Besa 7.92 cal. MG.

Examples Preserved.

III	T16065	1940	Tank	Brit. Army	RAC Museum, Bovington
Archer		1942		Brit. Army	RAC Museum, Bovington
Scissors		1944		Brit. Army	RAC Museum, Bovington

VALIANT

Designed by Vickers was the Valiant, a 1944 example of which is illustrated here.

(K. A. Jenkinson)

Towards the end of 1943, Vickers were investigating a design for an infantry tank in the form of an improved version of the Valentine. This resulted in the A38 design being born, named the Valiant which, whilst using as many existing Valentine components as possible, would incorporate a larger turret to accomodate a crew of three. To leave Vickers free for other work, detail design parentage was passed over to Birmingham Railway Carriage & Wagon Works who in turn, quickly passed this to Ruston & Hornsby who completed the pilot model in 1944. This used a GMC 210 hp. diesel engine which during field testing proved too slow. To overcome this problem, the second prototype named the Valiant II used a Rolls Royce Meteorite 8-cylinder engine. By this time however, the war was drawing to a close and in view of this the A38 was discontinued with no further vehicles being built. Armed with 1×75 mm. OQF and 2×7.92 cal. Besa MG, the Valiant was 17 ft. 7 in. long, 9 ft. 3 in. wide and 7 ft. 0 in. high.

Example Preserved.

1944   Tank   Brit. Army   RAC Museum, Bovington

VICKERS WHEEL-CUM-TRACK

Track troubles with the Medium tank led to experiments with a wheel-cum-track design. In the Medium tank the wheels were raised and lowered by means of a power take-off from the gearbox, this proving unsatisfactory since the balance of the tank was upset and excessive pitching resulted. A similar idea was developed by Vickers in their wheel-cum-track design, but this differed in principle in that the wheel suspension was rigidly attached to the hull. The track frames were mounted in vertical guides so that they could be raised of lowered by a power take-off operating through bell cranks. An experimental wheel-cum-track was built in 1928 but after testing, the design was abandoned.

Example Preserved.

ML8719	1928	Tank	Brit. Army	RAC Museum, Bovington

VOLKSWAGEN kdF

Popularly known as the Kubelwagen, the Volkswagen KdF was widely used by the German Forces during World War II. 999EMW shown here carries authentic German markings.

(K. A. Jenkinson)

The Volkswagen KdF was a 4×2 light car popularly known as the Kubelwagen. Introduced in 1939 it had a wheelbase of 2400 mm. and was powered by a Volkswagen 985 cc., 4-cylinder petrol engine. Transmission was via a 4-speed gearbox with limited-slip diff. whilst the brakes were mechanically operated. In March 1943, the original engine was replaced in production by a 1131 cc. Volkswagen 4-cylinder unit and the KdF remained in production until 1945 by which time around 52,000 had been built.

Examples Preserved.

	1941	Light Car	Germ. Army	Pearce, Holywell
WNJ894H	1942	Light Car	Germ. Army	Dobson, Lewes

188

	1942	Light Car	Germ. Army	Olgiati, Surrey
	1942	Light Car	Germ. Army	Oliver, Eton Wick
999EMW	1943	Light Car	Germ. Army	Chapman, Norton
	1943	Light Car	Germ. Army	Mann, Lamanva
	1943	Light Car	Germ. Army	Kenton, London
	1943	Light Car	Germ. Army	Wheeler, Oxon
LMO898E	1944	Light Car	Germ. Army	Passey, Newbury
	1944	Light Car	Germ. Army	Pearson, Leicester
FCX314	1945	Light Car	Germ. Army	Dobson, Lewes

VOLKSWAGEN Kfz 1/20

Often referred to as the Schwimmwagen, the Volkswagen Kfz 1/20 was a 4×4 amphibious light car. Having a wheelbase of 6 ft. 6 in., it was powered by a Volkswagen 4-cylinder petrol engine and had a 5-speed gearbox. First produced in 1942, a total of 14,265 were built before the model was discontinued in 1944.

Examples Preserved.

	1942	Amphibian	Germ. Army	Kenton, London
	1943	Amphibian	Germ. Army	Oliver, Eton Wick
	1943	Amphibian	Germ. Army	Mann, Lamanva

WAFFENTRAGER

Now safely preserved for posterity is this German Waffentrager self-propelled gun.

(K. A. Jenkinson)

The prototype in the Waffentrager series of self-propelled guns, this experimental dismountable self-propelled gun was installed by Krupp in 1942. Being a 105 mm. Howitzer, it is mounted on a modified PzKpfw IV medium tank chassis, powered by a Maybach V12 in-line petrol engine. Built in experimental form, it was modified and re-classified before entering full production.

Example Preserved.

1942 S.P. Gun	Germ. Army	Imperial War Museum, London

WARD LaFRANCE 'M1A1' 1000 series

The huge size of the Ward LaFrance 1000 series 5 heavy wrecker is illustrated in CFT396V, seen here immaculately restored.

(K. A. Jenkinson)

The Ward LaFrance M1A1 1000 series 5 was introduced in 1943, being developed from the M1 first produced in 1940. A 6-ton 6×6 heavy wrecker, it was of normal control layout and featured an open cab. Having a wheelbase of 15 ft. 1 in., it was powered by a Continental 6-cylinder petrol engine of 145 bhp. and had a 5-speed gearbox with 2-speed transfer box, its brakes being air operated. It was fitted with a 5-ton swinging-boom crane and the M1A1 was also produced to the same specification by Kenworth, both makes remaining in production until 1945.

Examples Preserved.

CFT396V	1943	Heavy Wrecker	US Army	Bowman, Blaydon
	1943	Heavy Wrecker		Wallsgrove, Warwicks

WHIPPET

The Mark A Whippet medium tank, built by Fosters of Lincoln, first went into production in 1918. Powered by 2 Tylor 6-cylinder petrol tractor engines, each developing 45 hp., and the bogies were unsprung. Designed for a crew of 3, the Whippet was 20 ft. 0 in. long, 8 ft. 7 in. wide and 9 ft. 0 in. high. It was armed with 4×.303 in. Hotchkiss MG's. Around 200 were built in 1918 before the design was discontinued and almost all were scrapped the following year.

Example Preserved.

	1918	Tank	Brit. Army	RAC Museum, Bovington

WHITE M3A1

This M3A1 built for the U.S. Army was one of many armoured scout cars built to this design in World War II.

(K. A. Jenkinson)

First appearing in 1940, the White M3A1 was built in the U.S. as a 4×4 armoured scout car of normal control design. Given a wheelbase of 10 ft. 11 in., it uses a Hercules JXD 6-cylinder petrol engine of 5.24 litres capacity with a bore and stroke of 4 in.×4¼ in. Alternative engines used were a Hercules 6-cylinder DJXD diesel unit and a Buda 6-cylinder diesel engine. Transmission is via a 4-speed gearbox with 2-speed auxiliary box with no provision for disconnecting front wheel drive whilst the axles are of the fully floating type with spiral bevel drive. Its bodywork, in which seating is provided for the driver and 7 passengers is of ¼ in. armour plate with a ½ in. front screen and the windscreen has an armour plate flap which can be lowered to totally cover it. A Browning machine gun be mounted. When used by the British and Canadian armies, the M3A1 also served as a personnel carrier, command car and ambulance. It remained in production until 1945.

Examples Preserved.

NUL535P	Scout Car	Stillwood, London
	Scout Car	Wilkinson, St. Albans
	Scout Car	Halsall, Guildford
27248	Scout Car	Oliver, Egham
	Scout Car	Warnham War Museum
2058772	Scout Car	Mann, Lamanva
	Scout Car	Bowman, Blaydon

WHITE M3A2

JGF849S, a White M3A2 half-track restored to original condition is seen here complete with its American markings.

(K. A. Jenkinson)

The M3A2 was built by White, Autocar, International Harvester and Diamond T and was introduced in April 1943. The M3A2 was a normal control half-track vehicle which could be used as a personnel carrier, gun tower or mortar carrier. Powered by a 6-cylinder petrol engine of either White, Diamond T or International manufacture, it had a 4-speed gearbox with 2-speed transfer box and hydrovac brakes. Its wheelbase was 11 ft. 3½ in. and it was designed to carry 13 men. The M3A2 never entered full production however and its design was dropped later in 1943.

Examples Preserved.

GNK895T	1943	Personnel Carrier		Beddall, Iver
	1943	Personnel Carrier	US Army	Warnham War Museum
	1943	Personnel Carrier	US Army	Gray, Worthing
JGF8495	1943	Personnel Carrier	US Army	Mann, Lamanva

WILLYS M38

The differences between the Willys MB and the M38 can be clearly seen in this view of the latter at Durham in 1980.

(K. A. Jenkinson)

The Willys M38 jeep introduced in 1947 was basically a replacement for the remaining World War II jeeps still in service. Given a wheelbase of 6 ft. 8 in., it was powered by a 4-cylinder petrol engine of 65 bhp. and had a 3-speed gearbox with 2-speed transfer box and hydraulic brakes. An improved 24-volt electrical system was fitted as was better weather protection and deep water fording equipment. A total of 60,345 were built before production ended in 1952.

Examples Preserved.

JDP885N	1947	Jeep		Laver, Shepperton
	1951	Jeep	US Army	Begg, Stanley

WILLYS M38A1

Not restored when photographed here, this Willys M38A1 is seen in the condition in which it was acquired.

(K. A. Jenkinson)

Making its debut in 1952, the Willys M38A1 was basically an improved version of the M38 with a more powerful engine. Having a 6 ft. 9 in. wheelbase it was fitted with a 4-cylinder petrol engine of 72 bhp. and had a 3-speed gearbox with 2-speed transfer box and hydraulic brakes. It continued in production until the late 'fifties.

Example Preserved.

TWY871	1954	Jeep	Smith, Horbury

WILLYS CJ2A

Resembling the standard World War II jeep is ZE2409, a Willys CJ2A restored to its original state.
(G. Thompson)

The Willys CJ2A, first built in June 1945 was a ¼-ton 4×4 'jeep' of normal control layout. Having a wheelbase of 6 ft. 8 in. it was fitted with a 4-cylinder petrol engine of 71 bhp. and had a 3-speed gearbox with 2-speed transfer box. It had hydraulic brakes and remained in production until 1948, by which time 214,764 had been built.

Example Preserved.

ZE2409   1947   Jeep   Thompson, Newcastle

WILLYS MB

The famous Willys MB jeep is depicted here as a reminder of a once common type of military vehicle used by forces in many countries.

(K. A. Jenkinson)

Introduced in 1941, the U.S. built Willys MB jeep is a ¼-ton 4×4 model. Of normal control layout with a wheelbase of 6 ft. 8 in., it uses a Willys 4-cylinder petrol engine of 54 bhp. with a 3-speed gearbox and 2-speed transfer box. Hydraulic brakes act on all four wheels. Fitted with reconnaissance car/utility bodywork, the MB was used by the allied forces in almost every war theatre, and it remained in production until 1945 by which time a total 361,349 had been built.

Examples Preserved.

AFT153B	1941	Jeep	US Army	Quick, London
FF6555	1941	Jeep		Private Owner
JSB667G	1941	Jeep		Hayward, Coulsdon
USA848	1941	Jeep	US Army	Hargreaves, Keighley
936CBB	1941	Jeep	US Army	Hayden-Ritchie, Ryde
	1941	Jeep		Sanders, Farmoor
	1941	Jeep		Pearce, Holywell
	1941	Jeep		Ottewill, Somerset
	1941	Jeep	US Army	Shepard, Sturminster Newton
	1941	Jeep		Davis, Bristol
	1941	Jeep	US Army	Rowlinson, Sussex
	1941	Jeep		Luxton, Dorset
	1941	Jeep		Marlow, Northants
	1941	Jeep	US Army	Shaw, Wilts.
	1941	Jeep		Gates, London
	1941	Jeep		Fortnum, Warwick
BF0229	1942	Jeep		Mansell, Pershore
DBN81	1942	Jeep		Private Owner

WILLYS MB—*continued*

DJB623	1942	Jeep		Private Owner
HBP997H	1942	Jeep	US Army	Warnham War Museum
HCN72	1942	Jeep	US Army	Maslen, Enfield
HYD813	1942	Jeep		Busby & Houlahan, Hook Norton
	1942	Jeep		Stanley, Cramlington
EJM242	1942	Jeep		Taylor, Norton
	1942	Jeep		Robson, Wylam
OKN525	1942	Jeep	US Army	Private owner
WLK418	1942	Jeep		Baker, Wyverstone
44FPD	1942	Jeep	US Army	Warnham War Museum
	1942	Jeep	US Army	Trivett, Plymouth
	1942	Jeep		Fry, Barry
	1942	Jeep	US Army	Vernon, Lee on Solent
	1942	Jeep		Prouse, Melksham
	1942	Jeep	US Army	Rushton, Devon
	1942	Jeep	US Army	Chedzoy, Taunton
TFV230	1942	Jeep	US Army	Evans, Morcambe
	1942	Jeep		Busby, Shipston on Stour
	1942	Jeep		West, Surrey
	1942	Jeep	US Army	Willett, Rugby
	1942	Jeep	US Army	Millman, Devon
	1942	Jeep	US Army	Masters, Taunton
	1942	Jeep		Lewis, Staffs.
	1942	Jeep	US Army	Symonds, Exeter
	1942	Jeep	US Army	Standeven, Portishead
	1942	Jeep		Morgan, Prudhoe
	1942	Jeep		James, Glos.
	1942	Jeep	US Army	Burbidge, Jersey
	1942	Jeep	US Army	Miller, Lincoln
	1942	Jeep	US Army	Honeychurch, Salop.
664OWW	1942	Jeep		Dransfield, Horbury
	1942	Jeep		Gardiner, Sussex
	1942	Jeep		Weston, Salop.
	1942	Jeep		Kelly, London
GOP547	1942	Jeep	US Army	Young, Solihull
	1942	Jeep		LeGresley, Jersey
CFX90	1943	Jeep	US Army	Busby, Hook Norton
FWO957	1943	Jeep	US Army	Gray, Worthing
HXD150	1943	Jeep		Private Owner
5773U	1943	Jeep	Brit. Army	Moulson, Bradford
KCE509	1943	Jeep	US Army	Private owner
3211UT	1943	Jeep	US Army	Private owner
416HKP	1943	Jeep		Jackson, Lancaster
	1943	Jeep	US Army	Maddocks, Shrewsbury
	1943	Jeep		Rivers, Berks.
MXK572	1943	Jeep	Brit. Army	Bowman, Blaydon
	1943	Jeep	US Army	Roberts, Salop.
	1943	Jeep	US Army	Thompson, Gwent
	1943	Jeep		Clarke, Leamington
	1943	Jeep		Harper, Hereford
HNK962	1943	Jeep		Spinks, Walsall
	1943	Jeep	US Army	Milton, Pontypridd
	1943	Jeep	US Army	Wallis, Bucks.
	1943	Jeep		Fortnum, Warwick

833BUO	1943	Jeep	US Army	Simpson, Horbury
	1943	Jeep		Ramsey, London
EMR309	1943	Jeep	US Army	Private Owner
LHK634	1943	Jeep		Brooks, Old Heathfield
OFY498	1943	Jeep	US Army	Pickles, Kirkham
XPT203	1943	Jeep	US Army	Roberts, Kidderminster
	1943	Jeep		Alexander, Bournemouth
	1943	Jeep		Toone, Rustington
	1943	Jeep		McMillan, Falkirk
	1943	Jeep		Taylor, Consett
102GKM	1943	Jeep	US Army	Private Owner
	1943	Jeep		Orchard, Devizes
PUO674	1943	Jeep		Winter, Portishead
	1943	Jeep		Mann, Lamanva
	1943	Jeep	US Army	Wyer, Warminster
	1943	Jeep		Cleaver, Chadlington
	1943	Jeep		Jones, Bridgend
	1943	Jeep		Halsall, Guildford
	1943	Jeep		Angel, Stroud
UXT929	1943	Jeep	US Army	Lindhurst, Warnham
XPT834L	1943	Jeep	US Army	Ashton, Sedgefield
	1943	Jeep		Tidey, Devon
	1943	Jeep	US Army	Wirth, Kent
	1943	Jeep	US Army	Broadway, Wilts.
	1943	Jeep		Bellis, Lancaster
	1943	Jeep	US Army	Park, Aberdeen
	1943	Jeep		Hughes, Bristol
TWP724	1943	Jeep	US Army	Private Owner
UDF181	1943	Jeep	Brit. Army	Monahan, Sale
5149E	1943	Jeep		Private Owner
EPR241	1944	Jeep		National Motor Museum, Beaulieu
	1944	Jeep	US Army	Pascoe, Southsea
	1944	Jeep	US Army	James, Glos.
	1944	Jeep		Groombridge, Heathfield
	1944	Jeep	US Army	Short, Dorset
KKX712	1944	Jeep		Stocker, Ruislip
MKX140	1944	Jeep		Bone, Seaford
XPT133	1944	Jeep	US Army	Elgey, Durham
	1944	Jeep		Davidson, Edinburgh
	1944	Jeep		Booth, Mold
	1944	Jeep		Hickman, Worcs.
891PTJ	1944	Jeep	US Army	Dransfield, Horbury
	1944	Jeep		Meadmore, Surrey
	1944	Jeep		Hamilton, Stirling
	1944	Jeep		Mitchell, London
CEA641	1944	Jeep		Daniels, Market Drayton
	1944	Jeep	US Army	Passey, Newbury
	1944	Jeep		Davies, Dinas Powis
61FTD	1944	Jeep	US Army	Osborne, Saffron Walden
102GKM	1944	Jeep		Brooks, Old Heathfield
	1944	Jeep	US Army	Lazenby, Oxford
	1944	Jeep		Rowland, London
	1944	Jeep		Winchcombe, Wilts.
	1944	Jeep	US Army	Huntley, Hants.
	1944	Jeep	US Army	Johnson, Berks.
NTL261	1945	Jeep	US Army	Bickle, Whickham

1945	Jeep		Ellis, Reading
1945	Jeep		Antrobus, Wilts
1945	Jeep	US Army	Coote, Cornwall
1945	Jeep	US Army	Barton, London
1945	Jeep	US Army	Mann, Lamanva
1945	Jeep		Scott, Beckenham

WINDSOR CARRIER

Authentically restored to 'as new' condition is this Ford Windsor Carrier.

(P. Isaac)

The Ford C49WC Windsor Carrier was introduced in 1944 as an enlarged development of the Universal Carrier. Having a length of 14 ft. 4½ in., width of 6 ft. 11 in. and height of 4 ft. 9½ in., the Windsor was powered by a Ford V8 30 hp petrol engine and had a 4-speed gearbox and 2-speed transfer box. Armed with a Bren gun, it was a fully tracked vehicle built by Ford in Canada using hulls made by the Canadian Bridge Co. Over 5,000 were built before production ceased in 1945.

Example Preserved.

T286185　1945　Personnel Carrier　Brit. Army　Isaac, Umberleigh

WOLSELEY CR

The only survivor of the Wolseley lorries built prior to World War I is LE5740, this W.D. example dating from 1912.

(R. F. Mack)

The Wolseley CR was first introduced in 1912. Of normal control layout, it was built to carry a capacity of 70 cwt. and was powered by a Wolseley 33.96 hp 4-cylinder petrol engine with a bore and stroke of 117 mm. × 130 mm. A 4-speed gearbox was used whilst the rear axle had bevel final drive. The CR was a subsidy model and remained in production until 1915.

Example Preserved.

LE5470	1912	G/S Lorry	War Dept.	Akehurst, Gillingham

INDEX